LIGHT

A LANGUAGE OF CELEBRATION

by

KENT E. SCHNEIDER

and

SISTER ADELAIDE ORTEGEL

Published by

THE CENTER FOR CONTEMPORARY CELEBRATION . CHICAGO, ILLIN

Designed and Illustrated by Sister Adelaide Ortegel, S.P.

Photography by Robert Wells

Other photographs by:

    Rev. Richard Woods, O.P., p. 8
    Sister Adelaide, S.P., p. 39, 86, 90, 108, 117
    Bob Black, p. 66
    Mary Alice DeRose, p. 80, 81
    Tom Kieft, p. 82
    Kent Schneider, p. 83
    Lorrayne Hockman, p. 131
    Sister Mary Lucas, back cover

Special Thanks:

    to the people who contributed financially to give us
    the time to write and publish this book

    and to Sandra Assarian, Sister Cathy Campbell and
    Sister Joureene Pannier for helping us prepare the
    manuscript.

first connections

To search into the meaning of LIGHT

                    is to delve into mystery.

          I strike a match in darkness.

          I see!
                    just a foot beyond my nose.

          MORE LIGHT! I shout.

          MORE!

          The boundaries push back to let me see
          How much more LIGHT
                              I need.

I'm afraid of the dark, but suspicious of the light.

Woody Allen

We are creatures of light.
We depend upon it for life and growth.
It is just as much one of the primal phenomena of this world
for us, as it was for early man.

The ancient Egyptians personified the mystery of LIGHT and its
life-giving powers in the sun-god, ATEN. The illustration below
is adapted from a limestone relief, c. 1355 B.C. in the Aten
Temple at Tell el Amarna, Egypt. King Akhenaten and his Queen
are making sacrificial offerings to ATEN. The power of the
sun-disc is depicted with radiating arms reaching to bestow
vital forces symbolized by the ANKH, hieroglyph for enduring
life. The ANKH is held to the nostrils of the royal couple
in order that the life-giving forces might be inhaled.

YOU WILL KNOW THE LIGHT TO THE DEGREE YOU PARTICIPATE IN IT.

Let there be light!

the keynote
        of creation
for the ancient Hebrews.

God created the light
and the darkness.
Darkness is more than
the absence of light.
It is from the womb of
darkness and chaos that
existence is brought
forth.

Light uncovers and
quickens to life that
which is hidden in
darkness.

Light and darkness
must co-exist in this
world. Both are
energies in tension.
The conflict is a
ceaseless one.

Christ used the natural symbolism of LIGHT to help us understand
his work among us.

Once, not long before his death, he was asked:

Who is the Son of Man?

He answered:

> *The light will be with you only a little longer now.*
> *Walk, while you have the light,*
> *or the dark will overtake you:*
> *he who walks in the dark does not know where he is going.*
> *While you still have the light,*
> *believe in the light*
> *and you will become sons of light.*
>   *John 12:36*

Christ gave no further explanation. Like his friends, we are
left to search out the meaning:

LIGHT has a centering influence. Like a magnet, one candle
burning in the dark can capture the whole of our attention and
draw together our powers of thought. It holds people together
in a circle of warmth. It can dispel darkness, yet the darkness
has no power to overcome it unless the light weakens. It is a
presence affecting all around it.

> Light can be shared
>   yet is never diminished,
>
>   cherished
>   but never entirely contained,
>
>   reflected, absorbed
>   yet, in itself, remains the same.

> *All that came to be had life in him*
> *and that life was the light of men,*
> *a light that shines in the dark*
> *a light that darkness could not overpower.*
>   *John 1:4-5*

9

Contemporary man knows a little bit more about the physical properties of LIGHT. It's interesting to relate the scientific knowledge with the earlier understandings and symbolism.

LIGHT is energy—generated inside an atom in the sun or fire or a light bulb. It can be controlled to a certain extent, made to work for man, but its mystery still cannot be fully penetrated.

LIGHT is both the conveyor of the message and the message itself. It reveals the world to us. It also speaks to us by its very presence. This idea needs further probing:

Think of the amount of sensory data that comes to us by way of LIGHT—

All that we see—all color, shape, pattern, texture, motion—all that we read.

It is through the interaction of light waves with
   objects in the world around us that we are able
   to perceive with our eyes.

Sensations of warmth—infrared and ultraviolet
   waves—are perceived by our skin. We call it
   heat.

Strange to say, we even "hear" light energy since
   radio waves are physically the same as light waves,
   only longer.

Expand all of the sensory data by the multi-dimensions of films,
television, videotape, satellite and laser beam. Through the
technology of light we can have instant communication on a global level—in living color.

Now, let's look at LIGHT itself as MESSAGE, as intensity of
meaning that can pierce into our consciousness:

Light addresses us.

      Like moths we are drawn to it.
      Maybe it is our homing instinct.
      Like family members we gather in the tradition of
         "Keep the Home Fires Burning"

      Flashing lights
         -warning signal or protecting guide
         -bringing reassurance
         -a glint of hope seen at the end of a dark tunnel

      Fireworks
         -anticipating the first dazzling burst
         -for a few brief seconds a whole stadium of people
            inhale the cascade of light.

      Pre-dawn
         -straining for the sun's first breakthrough
         -birth of fresh hope and limitless possibilities
         -the light-full unfolding of a new day

FOCUSING FOR LIGHT

> In photography FOCUSING *is the*
> *process of adjusting the lens*
> *in order to clarify the image.*
> Without focus the picture will
> be blurred.

> FOCUSING *is centering upon an image or an*
> *idea until it becomes* <u>*in-sight-full,*</u> *the*
> *fullness of visioning.*

We hope that "LIGHT: A LANGUAGE OF CELEBRATION" will present to
you the vocabulary--the tools, techniques and effects of the
language,

> and enable you to search beneath the surface for the
> unique expressiveness of light.

Every art has its own expressiveness. This is the quality that
makes it a language.

Each medium speaks something that cannot be said as well in any
other art form.

And so, when we work with LIGHT we are able to speak a new
Language of Vision, both artistically and prophetically.

Our ability to speak this language will depend upon how well
the understandings of the experiences in this book can be focused within the individual's style of creating. In other
words, this book is a book that is designed to be tried out,
not simply read about. For, like other types of knowledge,
a new language must be learned. Fluency comes with use.

"LIGHT: A LANGUAGE OF CELEBRATION" grows from our wide variety
of experiences in workshops which we have conducted all around
the country.

We share our ideas with you in the hope
that there are people who are interested
in projected light as one mode
of expressing feelings and faiths.

We offer these ideas for those people
who know the meaning of celebration's
ministry in the humanization of
the world.

May you grow in the
fullness of Light.

Kent and Adelaide

Part 1

KNOWING CELEBRATION

In this chapter, we share with you some of the insights and developing ideas we've experienced in designing workshops and in preparing celebrative events. However, celebration will not be fully understood merely by reading these pages. It is a pervading Spirit which cannot be contained in printed words—celebration dwells within people.

> Celebration is to be lived out
>   not just read about.
>
> It is to be experienced
>   not just explained.
>
> It will be known only to the degree
>   with which we participate.

There are two ways of knowing:

> to <u>go all around</u> and learn the breadth, height and length of the surface;
>
> to <u>enter in</u> and search the depth of that which you seek to know. You journey below the surface and enter the pulse. You go beyond the text's surface and into the texture.

The path of celebration is characterized by an <u>entering into invitation,</u> rather than a circular tour that stays a diameter's distance away from the center of life. Each of us must decide which path to chart and journey. But be aware of those who will come to you and simply want to enter in a little way:

> There once were three men who came to a little room where a wise man was reading from the Book of Life. One of the three men explained that they had journeyed to see the wise man so that they could enter into his presence and read the Book of Life. The wise man asked: "How far do you want to come in to the knowledge of living?" The three men conferred with one another. Then one of them said, "Just far enough so that we can say we've been there."

Life is too crucial to allow those who seek status to shape
society. People around the world are tired of being the con-
sumer victims of the "high price and hard sell" style. There
is an ever-growing consciousness that man's destiny is as
creative shaper of livable alternatives. People have become
fed-up with big party-bosses, education that has the quality
of sausage-stuffing and our culture's frantic pursuit of aliena-
tion. They are crying out against polluted atmospheres of rage,
hatred, death wishes for mankind and wealthy, immovable institu-
tions that neither say nor do anything.

In the midst of the mounting counter-culture is a growing
resurgence of religious feeling. Celebration is one of the
effective expressions of this Spirit now moving throughout the
world in a grass roots style rather than by hierarchical decree.
People are tired of being programmed.

As the staff of The Center has traveled throughout the country,
we have met people of all ages who are choosing to become expressive of God's Presence in the world with fascinating
imagery, fresh sounds, movement and kinetic visions. This is a
refreshening from the boredom of dead verbalisms and stagnant
structures. Churches are now beginning to listen to how the
Spirit of Celebration can enable the development of a people's
creativity.

DEVELOPING MEANINGS OF CELEBRATION

Celebration has become one of our culturally used and abused words. It has been applied to mean grand openings, special sales, rock festivals and campus carnivals, religious services, recordings ("Celebrate, Celebrate, Dance to the Music") and has been the title for numerous books and magazine articles. It is no wonder that people are often confused as to the meaning and content of celebration.

The Church has not ventured very far into celebrative style despite recent declarations by major church bodies to "be inspired and sustained through the celebration of our faith." For churches, celebration is a word too often employed and not often enjoyed. We have encountered many churches that are worshipping in the same mood and style that they've used for the last fifty years—but now they <u>call</u> it "celebration". Other groups feel that "celebration" means an occasional prettifying of the liturgy (to make it more interesting)—a guitar group, occasional folk song, dramatic reading or conversational sermon.

Some people think that celebration is just something that happens:
> We conducted a workshop in which a group of seminarians opposed the idea of preparing for a celebration. They felt that all you needed to do was to get together a rock band, bottles and people and with their own kinds of highs—and let it "happen".

Celebration should not be confused with "happening", which takes place without time and without sense of antecedent, kairos or future. The roots of celebration lie deep within the soil of heritage and form a framework for interpreting the breaking out of kairos in our midst. The momentum of celebration builds a people together in the face of adversity rather than segmenting and separating. There is the sense that human persons are involved and not supervised mannikins.

Celebration is more complex than just dealing with the "happy things" of life. Too many so-called "celebrations" attempt to give everyone a pseudo-joy which never really takes hold. The planners of the service are too tightly glued to printed bulletins. Cries of "Rejoice!" "Let's Celebrate!" and "Alleluia!" become confessions of the lack of trust and enthusiasm, rather than proclamations of living.

One of the most difficult concepts for people to grasp is that celebration involves an entering into the agony as well as the triumph of life. The major use of "celebrate" in religious communities occurs in such phrases as "celebrate the Mass" (the Divine Mysteries) or "celebrate the Lord's Supper" (Communion or the Eucharist) and "celebrate the Sabbath" (when life returns to its place of peace in the universe from the agony and idolatry of existence).

We celebrate in the presence of awesome mystery—which includes not only the mystery of living but also the mystery of suffering and death in the midst of creation.

CELEBRATION is the Inter-Play-Ground
of God's Animating Spirit
and Man's Response to His Presence

The Spirit, this animating energy of life, invades our daily existence, transforming the common episodes of daily-ness into uncommon moments of meaning.

As a Spirit energy within and without man, the presence of celebration is not predictable, not a repeatable commodity. Rather, it is an event that moves within a cluster of people. It is extraordinary, memorable and unique. Spirit sets a precedent.

> A small group of people, very concerned about the future of love in the world, met together in one room. They talked of the New Life they had known for a few years. They became convinced that they must make it known even if it meant suffering and imprisonment. They could not give up speaking of the things they had seen and heard and believed would come. As they talked, they were suddenly empowered as by a strong, driving wind, full of sound, loud and deep. And immediately, all mankind was embraced in their love and concern. They each began to speak boldly with the result that every man could understand in his own language that a Day of Promise had come.

In the world's mix of good and destruction, of joy and sorrow, of creation and catastrophe, celebration is a way by which a people who trust each other and gather to speak a common language can make sense out of such a world. And in the process we come to a clarification of ourselves and the people with whom we live.

Celebration is a way of journeying through the world with a convictional belief that enables us to act with conscience. If the truth in which we participate has meaning, it must take form within us at each moment.

> I cannot be still.
> As long as someone is hungry
> I cannot be full.
> As long as someone is poor
> I cannot be rich.
> As long as someone is prisoner
> I cannot be free.

Celebration is taking in both the guilt and the triumph of this day in offering to God who still transforms the world.

CELEBRATION is the action of COME-UNITY among a people who trust each other enough to risk themselves in expressiveness.

Celebrating is not the act of one person, since a person in isolated aloneness cannot celebrate. Nor, is celebration the responsibility of the minister or priest alone. If it is to have meaning, it will be "the work of the people" (liturgy) and will grow from the experiences they are sharing.

People often ask, "Do you have to have a COMMUNITY before you can celebrate, or does celebration build its own COMMUNITY?" There is no single answer to this probe since each celebrative event will present a new situation and therefore necessitate different preparations.

> We did a celebration in jazz for an ecumenical cluster of churches in Indiana. As the pews filled with more than 500 people, it could be sensed that many of them sat "isolated" from one another. We asked, "Do you know one another?" The people were invited to get to know those around them. The room then became

alive with people in friendly conversation,
rather than people sitting and waiting for the
service to begin.

There needs to be a movement of awareness and conviction flowing—
the sensing that a "new people is being born"— a people who have
potency to deal with the world we are in.

In developing celebrations we are asking questions:

What difference will it make in the world that
this people has been together?

What are the crossroads of struggle and decision
facing us?

Where is the freshness of freedom and opportunity
being offered?

Where is the Christ being crucified and rising up
in our world?

What is it that we might proclaim?

What is moving within our time that is worth stak-
ing our living on?

It is this quality of <u>peopleness</u> that is necessary content for
any celebration. <u>People are our best resources for celebrating</u>.

To participate in communal-religious-celebration, a person must
have the sense of <u>being with</u> and not just <u>alongside</u> this people.
There will be no celebrative quality if the person feels alien.
There must be opportunity for the expressiveness of each person
to be received.

It is the power and breadth of this gradually growing corporate
network of persons that gives the <u>enthusiasm</u> (*Greek: en-theos-
iasmos, to be filled with god*) to celebration. Within this network grows the freedom feeling that it is O.K. to be myself.
There is a hope for authenticity that builds as trust increases.

CELEBRATION IS THE

AGORA

FOR THE TRADITION AND THE CONTEMPORARY

Celebration is like a seed
that is planted in the soil of tradition.
This seed sends its roots
into the soil.
From these roots come new shoots
that give forth flowers and fruits
and more seeds.

But all this would not be possible unless
the seed was first planted in the soil of
TRADITION.

One of the prevalent attitudes we
encounter is the feeling that the CONTEMPORARY
is suspect because it is of the moment and,
therefore, temporary; while TRADITION is the
"accepted" way built on recitals of the past
(usually dead verbalisms of 18th and 19th
Century past).

Most churches, rather than seeing the
AGORA or MEETING PLACE of the contemporary and the tradition, put these
two qualities of our heritage at
opposite ends of the liturgical spectrum. Many places will have a 9 a.m.
"contemporary family service" and an
11 a.m. "traditional service". This
is an unnecessary split in community
life.

THE CONTEMPORARY AND THE TRADITIONAL
ARE BOTH OF THE SAME MOVEMENT

They are not polarities. The tradition is a journey that has
moved through history, is moving now, and will future a people.
The tradition is the aliveness of people, the pulse. The contemporary is the new wave of tradition. It is not "experimental"—
to be tried and discarded. Nor, is it the "radical". The contemporary is the broadening of the tradition. It is that unique
gift which our generation can make to our children, so that the
tradition is living and not a museum piece.

TRADITION is the bodied people.

CONTEMPORARY is the pulse of the moment.

Neither can be ignored; neither can stand alone.
To exclude the contemporary from the tradition is like never
preparing the soil for the seed. The ground becomes hard and
dry cracks appear. To think that the contemporary can stand
alone without the foundationing of the tradition is like cutting
off the new flower from its roots. The flower has no future.
Though pretty today, it will wither and die tomorrow.

Celebration is not a one-shot event.
It is the continuing dialogue with the past and the expectancy
of the future breaking out with clarity in the meeting place
(AGORA) of the present.

TUNING IN

"RELIGIOUS" CELEBRATION is the distinctive way of "tuning in"
to the world by people who choose to live with authenticity.
Rather than the ascribing to a set of beliefs or a memorized
creedal affirmation, being "RELIGIOUS" is actualizing your con-
victions.

By "RELIGIOUS" we do not mean something that necessarily happens in a church service, or an experience that is a separate sacred category. <u>To be RELIGIOUS is to be ACTUAL.</u>

It is recognizing that God's Presence with us is not as a "timekeeper" who has set the earth in motion and now separates himself from existence. God is in the midst of the world, sharing in the suffering and life of all men.

A description of RELIGIOUS CELEBRATION could include:

- the invitation to "enter in" to the depths of life, not just the surface.

- the story and journey with life-and-death-for-all-men significance which characterizes any person who is a part of the celebrating people.

- being in touch with the Creating Ground, the animating energy which makes life possible, opens futures and transforms the actual. Celebration is not something we do for ourselves but <u>for the sake of the world.</u>

- meeting something other than just our own emotions and glandular excitement.

- sharing the Christ life in an eventful way rather than letting Jesus be an external forgiver.

- a compelling, evocative, artistic speaking of God's engaging with man to create and transform man's situation. We take on the news of this day and try to make sense out of it.

- sensing the Depth of Mystery welling up in a people in moments of quiet, reflection, contemplation.

- offering ourselves by participating and shaping the events of our time with responsible freedom.

<u>Communal-Religious-Celebration is the liturgy of a people only when it enables the</u>

INDIVIDUATION of a person.

"Communal" does not mean that we all do the same thing. Too many liturgies encourage passivity and blind obedience. Everything is done <u>to</u> the people. Nor should "communal" mean that we try to develop services that "reach all the people" if it means that we make worship like a cafeteria serial line catering to individualists.

Celebration involves the jextapositioning of the whole community and the inner dimension of the individual. All of life is this <u>flow between</u> being with others and being within ourselves. We cannot be fully human without this interplay. If we are totally outside ourselves and hollow within, we really have nothing to offer others; and, if we live exclusively inside, we have no way of getting beyond.

> Jesus told us to love ourselves and to love
> our neighbors. He understood the abyss into
> which man plunges when he fails to be concerned
> enough about himself to discover his destiny.
> And man's destiny will only be realized in rela-
> tion to other people.

Celebration must encourage INDIVIDUATION, **not** "individualism". Some services feature musicians or ministers who come off more like "performers" than "enablers". They communicate a feeling that they are more pre-occupied with themselves than with the gathered community. It is hard to pin-point why it happens in certain situations and not in others. A hunch might be:

INDIVIDUALISM is an unfortunate self-centered style
in liturgy where one seeks to promote his own views and
talents without regard for others. The person gives the
impression that he is among the "elect" and his is the
<u>only</u> way.

The INDIVIDUATED person realizes that while he is not
his own creator, he <u>is</u> an agent of creation in the world.
He appreciates his own abilities in relation to the abilities and views of others. He sees his uniqueness as an
opportunity for giving.

Another hunch:

INDIVIDUALISM is characteristic of those who would admire Jesus—people who stand off at a distance and spectate. They want to get in on the action, but not too far in. They have things to great importance to do. Like the rich young man, or the son who had to bury his father, they cannot follow.

The INDIVIDUATED person has a distinctive quality of contributing experience, powers and understandings to a group. The person is a <u>follower</u> of Jesus— with both backbone and muscle. He has the commitment and resoluteness to carry through his vocation even if the crowd is afraid to. He knows the taste of freedom because he knows the God in whom to dwell <u>is</u> freedom.

What are some of the qualities of COMMUNAL-RELIGIOUS- CELEBRATION that provide for the

INDIVIDUATED PERSON?

In celebration we recognize the responsibility each person has for what has been done or not done. This is a traditional stance for confession—the realization of one's answerability to God.

Celebration must include opportunities for the person to tune in to the uniqueness which <u>is</u> the person. This encourages us to develop meditation and contemplation as styles of celebration.

At some point in the flow of the liturgy, the New Person must be unforgettably expressed to the community. A model of becoming Christian which has a quality of implementation is articulated.

Celebration, since it grows from the experiences of this people, will awaken within each person a ministry of depth concern in which each member senses the meaning and mystery of the experiences and events of the day. Within this awakening is the originating God who gives a unity to our individuated characters.

CHARTING FOR CELEBRATION

chart: *a sheet giving information in a diagram
or table. A single outline map on which
information can be plotted or written.*

The Center for Contemporary Celebration has developed more than
300 different kinds of celebrations for churches, the city,
colleges, penitentiaries, YMCA Conferences, campers, religious
educators, street gangs, youth groups, high schools and hospitals.
And not one service went just as we had "planned". There was
always the unexpected innovation which emerged from the people
and became an important offering in the service. But this is
what. celebrative liturgy is all about--the work and sharings of
the people who gather.

So we have learned that you cannot plan for celebration's spontaneity, but you can prepare for it. It's much like making
preparations for a journey. You gather things that you antici-
pate you will need. You plot your travel, realizing that your
chart may be subject to revision depending on the needs of the
people with whom you journey.

The idea of CHARTING CELEBRATION is like mapping out new territory
to be explored. You will begin at a certain place and move with
all your resources, knowledge of the terrain and your wealth of
experiences to chart out a new land. To chart is not to experiment—a one shot event. It is a continuing expansion of awareness
of what it means to be in the world and in the midst of God. The
inroads and trail markings which your people have made will be
what you pass on to the next generation who will follow your path
or pioneer new trails.

In jazz, a chart is a sheet of music from which the band reads
and improvises. To it you bring your knowledge of the instrument,
your resources and your wealth of experiences to play out new
ideas. The chart usually gives the musicians the thematic,
rhythmic and harmonic parts and establishes the order of chord
progressions. It is within this ordering that the player has
the freedom to move.

CHARTING CELEBRATION also involves basic "progressions" around
which the people build and move. In designing celebration we
do not try to make things fit into an already established order.
This is like trying to program for the presence of Spirit. The
ordering will grow out of the meaning and experiences of the
community. What we do is to prepare pathways along which people
move through the liturgy. We offer many alternative routes or
modes of expression to our common destiny.

There are basic phases which communal-religious-celebration
utilizes for interweaving and flow. These are not segments already ordered for liturgy but essential feelings and styles which
occur and re-occur throughout each celebration.

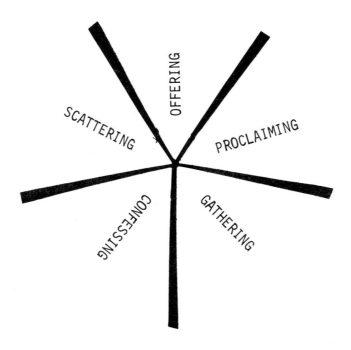

The design on the next two pages is one way of visualizing the
movement and inter-play of these basic phases. There is a
dynamic centering of ideas and yet a diversity of expressions.

GATHERING

PROCLAIMING

CONFESSING

OFFERING

SCATTERING

GATHERING is the re-membering into a people.

The way we begin is crucial. In some way the GATHERING must re-member this people. It should re-awaken a communal awareness of God's Presence, the heritage and the history-now-being-made, in which we all share. Rarely, if ever, do congregational readings/responses or "words of praise" adequately unite individuals, strangers and families into a People. The GATHERING should take in the fresh experiences and new meanings which this group has had since we were last together.

The visual environment is an important signal as to the style and meaning of celebration. New banners, original bulletin designs, light environments, slides and film all proclaim "We are a new people this day—we are not the same folks that came together last week—this is a new time and our environment symbolizes that freshness."

> We worked with a church community to design an Advent celebration. The people felt that they were tired of the Christmas wrappings and wanted to get down to some Christian rapping about the expectancy of Jesus' birth. How could we help people experience the commercial trash of the season (without having to talk about the tired subject)?

> The people who were preparing the celebration decided that the visual environment would be one of clutter, packages, the familiar Christmas wrapping paper strewn throughout the sanctuary and pews. As people came to the church that Sunday they were invited to take a broom or waste basket and help clear away the commercial camouflage and prepare for the Birth.

> This GATHERING worked very effectively to set the mood of the service. It also was a way of avoiding the "come, sit and wait" style of worship. When two or three are gathered, celebration begins.

The GATHERING needs to be a fresh focusing each time we meet. It must be authentic and a prelude to what is coming. It should not be a repeatable commodity from week to week.

In 1968, we did an Easter celebration in jazz. For this
event the preparations included: new hymns, six banners,
a bulletin cover design and a new liturgy. The banners
were unfurled as a dramatic offering to the congregation.
It was a memorable time.

However, three years later, the same banners are still
hanging. Visually, nothing fresh has been added in
the life of that congregation.

Like celebration, our styles of GATHERING should have a variety
to them. They should not have the quality of the repeatable
commodity. Nor should we try to s-t-r-e-t-c-h an idea to fit
all occasions.

The tone of GATHERING is one of warmth and welcome, not the cold
cathedral chills. In some way, people are made aware that they
and others are personally present and not painted on the pews.

PROCLAIMING is the event of God-with-us.

Proclaiming is a focal point in celebration—

God communing <u>with</u> and communicating <u>to</u> a people
who recognize the immediacy of this Presence.

No matter what form our proclamation takes (sermon, film, dance,
scripture, etc.) it should have the quality of "event". The
Hebrew mind used the word "dabar" to mean that words become
immediacy to be experienced, not just something to be read or
said. When they invoked—"in the name of God"—they sensed the
calling of God's Presence into their very midst. In our styles
of proclamation,we must strive for an immediacy quality, as if
the events of our heritage were understandably unfolding before
our eyes and ears.

PROCLAIMING is a <u>persistence-to-be-heard</u>. Its origins are deep
within creation. Like creation's first light, it is a focused
beam in the midst of swirling energy. In this directed focus

there is intensity and strength. If the light were diffused and scattered, it would be weak. This gives us some clues about preaching, which is in a difficult state of frustration and deterioration in many churches. Kierkegaard once wrote that preaching is the greatest art. The problem is that too many sermons try to say something about everything. Ministers must learn the art of appropriating what to say.

What we PROCLAIM must have an intensity, a focusing, rather than a weak diffusion which leads to confusion. We would seek to penetrate into the meaning of God's Presence in the midst of our daily experiences. While penetrating and in-sightful, PROCLAMATION also permits an opening of meanings. It enables a people to share their interiorities without fear of being put down for being honest.

PROCLAMATION has the quality of being a dialogue not a monologue. It deals with life experiences which are a part of this community and the Christian life. The PROCLAIMING is offered not for the praise or blame of one who speaks it or those who hear it. It is shared with the hope that the listener will become the witness-bearer and go and tell others.

CONFESSING is admitting the Christ to one another.

We are dealing with the wholeness of a person in celebration and not just with one segment. We deal with mind and intellect as well as feelings of hope and hurt. The CONFESSING is the input of the ambiguous nature of all life and human existence. It is both affirmation and realization that life is neither totally bad nor totally good and that we are called to decide and work with the real situation which is often the choice between lesser evils.

CONFESSION is choosing.

> "Behold, I set before you this day life and good, death and evil; therefore choose life. Choose you this day whom you will serve."

CONFESSING is living with answerable courage for the choices we have made.

We confess the shout of a prophetic "nevertheless" to prevalent stupidities, ambiguities, to comfort and fashion.
We choose to live.

CONFESSING carries the incognito liturgy which we encounter every day in the news and other media. It brings the awareness that Christ is our brother, dying and rising each moment of the day. We confess that our lives are inter-woven and that when one person suffers, the people suffer; and when one person is filled with joy, we co-enjoy together.

CONFESSION must be both individuating and communal. Our cele-bration must provide for the personal speaking as well as the community's voicing. The visually printed confession now used in many liturgies is not a very effective voicing for either the person or the community. Too often the printed confession asks people to respond with words they are not able to say with authenticity. No longer can a confession express the minister's private conviction as a model for everyone.

CONFESSION is an act of loving. It is the reconciliation of man with God in Jesus Christ. The PROCLAMATION comes that the disunion of ourselves with God, with other men, with the world and with ourselves is at an end. Man's origin is returned to him.

OFFERING is what we make, not something we take.

Celebration is participatory offering, a style of thanks-living which we do all the time. This idea is to be contrasted with an external gift or one which is made for just this occasion.
OFFERING is a continuing way of living with others and in God's Presence.

An OFFERING contains pulsing, human-life strands that sweep through all of life, passing through the experiences of each day and becoming more than they once were.

We offer <u>both</u> the broken-ness and whole-ness of this day to God for transformation—

        for whatever use may be served in the world

        for the development of good

        for clarification of ambiguities

        for the oneness of division

Our OFFERING is made in stark realism. This is what the day was, this is what we did and were—without hiddenness, without clothing what we present in fine words and phrases, untrue to reality.

We have found it helpful to put the meaning of the OFFERING into memorable images and movements. In the process of putting "this day" into symbol, we discover more what the experiences actually held. In sharing this day with others and God, we also compare the meaning of this moment with other moments of OFFERING in the Christian heritage and our own history. The meaning of "this day" is expanded by imaged future and recalled past.

    The minister asked if the people would move out of the pews and come forward to the altar and make the offering for this day. Gifts of poems, paintings, dollar bills, bread, wine, grapes were among the offerings brought to the altar as the congregation sang.

    A widow brought a trombone and laid it on the altar. Sensing the curiosity of the congregation, the minister asked the woman to explain the horn's meaning. "It had been my husband's horn," she said, "and he often played it in a brass choir in this church. I offer it this day in thanks to God for his life and talent and with the hope that some young person might use it to keep alive the tradition of good music in our congregation."

We pour our days of living into God for transformation. We move to the altar for alteration—the new possibility being given to mankind, to ourselves and to others sharing in the immediate event.

We offer the work of our hands for upbuilding the world, for passing it on to future generations. We realistically share in the death and creation that is our world and ourselves.

OFFERING is a kind of re-cycling, for we have been given much by God. In the receiving is also the giving—to actualize ourselves for the transformation of each day.

SCATTERING is the "Processional Benediction"

If "come, follow me" is one organizing image for our GATHERING, then the commissioning to "go into all the world" is what organizes our dispersal. Celebration does not cease when we leave each other—it continues, but now in different ways and in a multitude of places and people.

With the SCATTERING we are full with enthusiasm which means to be filled with God. We participate in creation's joyful shout of "I am!" Together, we are in the midst of experience and quality of life akin to that of God himself, who at the end of his first creation looked over the workings of his hands and felt it to be good. What we do in celebration may not be perfect, but we will feel that we have been pointing towards some values that are inherent for the living of human beings.

We now move from "creation's joy" to a confidence in our own work—that what we are about has a rightness and a readiness to be expressed even though the immediate society may not hear.

And because we have been a people together we will live with a resiliency. Life can bounce back from disaster and defeat. We see that the immediate difficulty is not the whole story of our destiny. For those who fully live, the future will bring other possibilities.

CHRIST TAKES FORM

kent schneider

This song has been used effectively at the end of communal celebrations. It is contagious enough that people will continue singing it as they scatter into the world.

Here's how we sing it:

The bass line begins first, sung by lower voices or men's voices.

Add the accompaniment of guitar, piano or organ; and begin to teach the melody line to the community.

As everyone starts getting into it, bring in a rehearsed choir of high voices.

The song should be sung with a solid rock drive to it.

Part 2

TOTAL ENVIRONMENT

Today there are people able to build environments of total world, life habitats of people around the world in one location, a collage of experiences never before available to one person simultaneously.

Contemporary communication's style is that of instantaneous world, a sensing of the multitude of possibilities in the moment. No longer are people hidden from one another. Minority groups can no longer be ignored. The environment invites commitment and participation. We have become involved with, and responsible for, a world manscape. The style of sequential living, where life comes one-thing-at-a-time, is passing. Our style is rapidly becoming a wholistic one where we view the causes and effects of our living in a one-hour TV special.

The present generation of emerging young adults, having grown-up on TV sets, is now expressing a totally new sensing of involvement in world events.

> Denied a voice in the 1968 Democratic Convention,
> young people began to infiltrate the party lines.
> Four years later the young people were able to be heard
> in Miami Beach. Even Mayor Daley felt their involvement.

The conscious style of many young people is as shapers of worlds of meaning, hope and depth. The once-labeled "Now Generation" no longer stands back and watches. They make things happen.

> Instead of rolling a hoop along a road, like the genera-
> tion before, this People gets inside the hoop and dances
> it. Art is no longer something to stand back and watch,
> it is now something which both the artist and the audi-
> ence create. Art becomes EVENT.

Life is no longer so neatly compartmentalized. It seems to flow within us and all around us. And with this total immersion into the stream of life has come the need for each person to develop skills of expression that give creation to the world.

A single finger below the surface

    breaks the calm of reflected past,

Like a pulse plunging into the waves of a world—

    foundationed by a rock that may

        never last.

Precariously perched, like his peers

    he peaks into the

        deep unknown.

Though I should walk in the valley of darkness
I will fear no evil.

Never before in history has man been so self-consciously aware
of his environment, yet so forlorn in the face of it. We have
a nostalgic longing for the simplicity of natural things, yet
we continually supplant· them with technological triumphs and
trivia.

Artificial, man-made things surround us, but not completely. The
rhythms of seasons and sun, storm and tides, blossom and seed,
inter-mingle with jet exhaust, super highways and central air
conditioning.

So we "perch precariously" and wander through the tall shadows
trying to understand ourselves in relation to "our world." We
can't just co-exist with environment; we live in inter-penetra-
tion. We engage it in conversation. Our inter-action with it
must be perceptible to us.

ENVIRONMENT is something to be shaped, as well as something
that shapes us. While it offers limitations to our space and
freedom; it also offers great potentialities. The question
is: Can man organize the environment to give meaning to life?

We are speaking now of more than physical surroundings. Environment includes the attitude man takes toward life, the way
he responds, and the good he values. Total environment embodies the pulse of life. Understanding the climate of this environment is a necessity for becoming a person. The word "climate" is used because it means: *any prevailing condition affecting life, activity, etc.*

Look again at the boy on the rock. If this were a stagnant
pond it could not support life. It could only decay and dry up.
But this is a lake replenished by fresh springs. There is movement and abundant life stirring beneath the surface.

If an environment becomes stagnant, rigid, repressive, it cannot give or receive life. Contemporary man's tension with the
environment is due to his inability to get back in phase with
this rhythm of inter-change. He has become victim of his own
victimization.

When our attitude to the world is cautious self-preservation
or apathetic acceptance, environment is little more than sterile
surfaces, stage scenery—ready-made, expendable:

> *As color-coded cables can create a calculation, so*
>   *the sleeping mind can parrot-off the phoney conversation.*
> *The programmed person cries about the weather yesterday:*
>   *another shorts his circuit and he wonders what he'll say.*

The need for imagination and creative alternatives is as crucial
as the need for unpolluted air and clean water.

When our longing is for opportunities to be fully human, to give
and receive life, we seek environments that will evoke and awaken
the spirit. We venture a closer look at the old environment and
alter it to bring forth fresh life.

The alter-ation may be as simple as a change of the seating arrangement, use of enlivening color, or a friendly greeting and
conversation, but it creates a new climate.

Here is an example of an environment designed for the celebration of the First Sunday of Lent:

In preparation, it was announced the previous Sunday that the next liturgy would be held in the dining hall. People were invited to bring pillows or blankets to sit on. An air of anticipation began to grow.

GATHERING

On the day itself, anticipation was heightened by the environment created for the event. Liquid sounds of electronic music mixed with the greetings of the people. The room was almost dark. An unusual seven foot wooden cross could be seen in flickering candlelight. In the center of the room stood a low eight foot long platform upon which rested two candles.

At the doorway each person was handed a long nail, a piece of paper, a crayon and one small song sheet.

The room filled quickly. People spread out blankets or pillows and sat down. Some chairs were available around the edges of the wall for those who might feel uncomfortable on the floor.

The liturgy began with one man, seated cross-legged on the platform, calling the people to awareness. He began with a quiet meditation, asking them to sense their own life force—their pulse—their breathing—their presence in a group.

PROCLAIMING

The candles were blown out. One single spotlight, hung from the ceiling, was projected on the platform and floor, lighting a circle of space for the dancers. The performance of four men and a woman depicted a stark embodiment of the power of evil crushing the spirit of freedom and love.

The four men were kneeling on the platform, doubled over like impenetrable rocks. The woman danced around them freely, almost playfully, trying to awake them. She was able to stir some reaction—then a bit of interest—

movement—reaching—as if they wished to accept her freedom gift. But the interest shifted to a desire for control. Slowly they engulfed her until she disappeared in their huge bulk. All that remained was the original rock-like form. (Blackout.)

CONFESSING

When the lights came up, the people were asked to think of instances from their own lives in which they had experienced this sort of engulfing. The dance had been so powerful that adults, as well as children, easily expressed their feelings by drawing pictures or symbols with the crayons and paper provided for them. These confessings were fastened to the wooden cross with nails. The song, "Were You There?" was sung.

OFFERING

The celebration continued with communion, a prayer for strength to do something about the conditions illustrated by the confessions, and the song, "Amazing Grace". The leader then asked the people to share any concerns they had. Open discussion, personal sharing and several songs characterized this moment.

SCATTERING

People did not want to leave one another. So the scattering took on the quality of on-goingness, rather than termination, as people moved the celebration into the streets with further conversation and song.

Small children, parents, teenagers, college students, older folks, had shared an experience of communal celebration within a special environment. They carried the intensity of concern right out with them. The various sense impressions introduced at the beginning were an integral part of the event. The old dining hall had become livable and life-giving human space for this special time.

The only lighting effects used were candles, the regular hall lights, a spotlight and darkness. These were employed with careful planning and timeing. The room would have been prosaic without the candles. The dramatic highpoint of the dance would have been lost without the circle of light and concluding darkness.

43

PROJECTING ENVIRONMENT

With LIGHT you can transform the givens of a room into personal significant space. Upon entering a room, messages, implications, memories, come to us from very small sensory clues. With the flick of a switch, projected environments can change the messages, over-lay implications and introduce different rememberings. The familiar becomes the unexpected.

The viewers are at the mercy of the projectionists, it's true. Some people will delight in this, others will feel threatened by it and want to put up protective defenses. It is necessary to be aware of these feelings. The planning stage should include ways of inviting people into the spirit of the new environment so that they can be creative participants.

Sometimes ideas are sparked by the very rooms available to you.

Here is an example:

> For the opening of a Lenten Workshop series, we wanted to take people on a journey through the desert. The journey would be a search for a clearer understanding of self in relation to others.
>
> The actual environment was an extensive church-school building. By exploring the place we discovered a large assembly hall, a variety of classrooms and an unusual circular tower room on the third floor. The tower room seemed to be the ideal place for the final sharing. We planned the sequence accordingly.
>
> A classroom with yellow walls and a beige rug needed only one slide projection to transform it into a barren desert. The slide image covered the entire wall. It focused the imagination, but not in a forced way. Each person could freely interpret "desert" and relate it to personal experiences. We gathered in this setting to prepare for the journey.

Why were we starting out?
Was it just a getting-away-from-the-fast-pace-of-life?
Or were we looking for something?
What extra baggage would we need to leave behind in
order to travel on?
It was important to allow enough time for the meditation
to become real, for the people to interact with the
space and with each other.

Light images in slides and films transport the meaning of the
world to focus on the inter-play-ground of man's soul.

The next part of the journey took us through dark corridors to the large assembly hall where a charcoal grill
provided the only light. The flickering glow spoke of
shelter and friendliness. Projection screens were ready
to re-gather the people in another kind of awareness.

Slide projections of faces looked out at us, one at a
time. Moments of frustration, belligerence, foolishness,
had been captured on film. These faces were not uncommon. They were like faces we see every day. We just
became more sensitive to them in this special context.
It gave us a chance to see our daily face-to-face
meetings in a different relationship. The people were
encouraged to carry on a communal dialogue with the
slide images. We responded with first impression and
then tried to get beneath the surface expressions on
the faces. The use of our own voices in conjunction
with the projected visual offered an unusual sensory
blend.

The climate of trust grows slowly.

Before long, thoughts were shared easily in the large
group. People were then invited to turn to a partner
and search out the face of the real person next to them.

Small pieces of charcoal were available so that we
might write down phrases, insights or ideas from our
conversations. Long sheets of mural paper had been
fastened to the wall for this purpose.

Each person could imprint something of self on the space that
had taken on new meaning.

Something of the environment (at least the smudge of charcoal) left its mark on the person. Candles were passed out and lighted for the last stage of the journey. Through dark corridors again and up stairways we made our way toward the upper room. Basins of water, soap and towels were waiting at the entryway for the pilgrims. The people washed and dried each others hands with the words, "Enter in—to the SPIRIT."

The combined candles of the group lighted the room. The sharing of water, bread, milk and honey brought the group together in a close bond of common understanding. There was a timeless mystery about that band of people meeting in the upper room. Some were able to express it in words, others preferred to let it sink in silently.

FLUID LIGHTS

Lights in fluid motion add another dimension to the possibilities of altering space.

FLUID LIGHTS are created with the OVERHEAD PROJECTOR and colored transparencies. Water or other liquids are used to produce the movement. The OVERHEAD lens projects such a wide area of light that walls and ceiling can be bathed in three-dimensional color— a kind of metamorphosis of space. The glow of the colors has something of the fascination we feel towards candlelight, but since it surrounds rather than centers, it calls for a different kind of participation.

By reflecting the color projection through a clear bowl of water, the dimension of movement is added. It could be called "light poetry." The pulsing inter-play of color IN-BODIES the viewer, painting an inner environment of light. It can take us beyond ourselves for a while, freeing the spirit and the powers of intuitive thought.

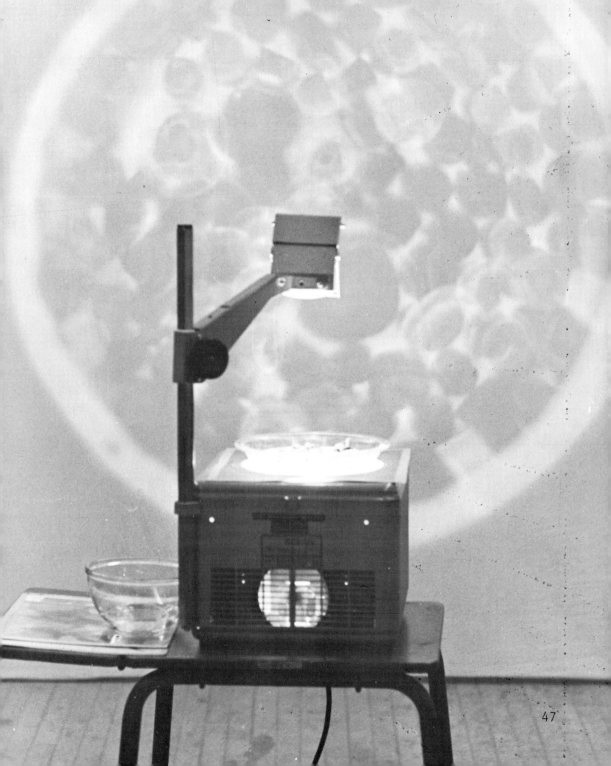

Part 3
OVERHEAD PROJECTION

The OVERHEAD PROJECTOR is the main piece of equipment needed for producing the special effects in a light environment. It is especially designed to project a large diameter screen area from a short distance.

KNOW YOUR OVERHEAD PROJECTOR

This is an essential step in the use of all electronic equipment. Know how to clean the lenses and to put in new bulbs. Clean, smooth-working projectors with safe wiring will prevent accidents and give dependable performance.

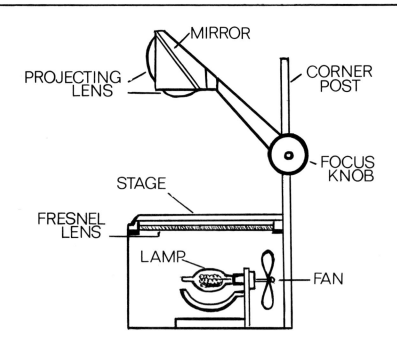

The BASIC PARTS of an OVERHEAD PROJECTOR

There are many types of OVERHEAD PROJECTORS. The one pictured on the preceding page is a light-weight model designed for school use. It has a STAGE area of 10 inches by 10 inches. The corner post arrangement allows for much greater facility in creating the different fluid effects. It is the most satisfactory type for light environment projection. You will notice that the photograph was taken in daylight. OVERHEADS project with great intensity and do not require complete darkness.

The TRANSPARENCIES used for projection can be made in countless ways. Sheets of clear acetate (.010 weight) cut slightly larger than the projection STAGE area (usually 11 in. square) are used as the basis for most of them.

PAINTED TRANSPARENCIES

When applied to clear acetate, materials like:

> Cryst-L-Craze
> Glass Stain
> Transparent Paint

project with intense color and surprising texture. Use the same methods as those described for SLIDE-MAKING. One additional technique is to sandwich the Cryst-L-Craze or other paints between two pieces of acetate. The brilliant color takes on a different kind of depth. If projected while still moist, bubbles move around in the heat of projection. When the transparency dries, bubble and ripple patterns remain. The paint does not crystallize.

LIVE PAINTINGS

For a fascinating visual treat, try painting the transparency while it is being projected on the OVERHEAD. Use syringes or droppers with the Cryst-L-Craze or other paints. It will appear as if you are squirting paint on the screen. If you move or tilt the acetate sheet, the colors will run together and inter-mix. The finished transparency becomes permanent when allowed to dry.

LINE DRAWINGS OR WRITING

Special felt-tip drawing pens are available for use on OVERHEAD transparencies. They should bear the indication: "Marks on Anything." India ink and a drawing pen will work on some kinds of acetate. Small lettering and fine detail drawing require the sharpness of the pen-point line. Song lyrics, responses and poems, as well as cartoons and intricate line drawings can all become part of the Light Expression.

ABSTRACT OVERLAY PATTERNS

Shapes can be cut or torn from colored acetate, cellophane or theatrical gels and lightly held in place with rubber cement on a clear acetate background. A protective cover sheet of clear acetate should be placed over the design and the edges bound with masking tape. Black silhouettes, lines or textures can be combined with the colored shapes. Use paper, yarn, string, net, lace, etc.

MOIRE PATTERNS

These OP-art patterns are made by overlaying precise repetitive figures so that their lines almost become superimposed. When placed on the STAGE of the OVERHEAD for projection every slight movement of the top sheet creates undulating flow waves. These patterns are used for science studies and can be purchased ready for projection. You can make your own moire' transparencies with India ink and drawing pens.

STENCIL projections for the OVERHEAD are simple, inexpensive and amazingly versatile. Dark construction paper or light-weight cardboard are the easiest to use. The design can be cut with scissors or an Xacto knife.

Shapes have a language of their own. Experiment with the different moods they can create:

PAPER STENCILS can be used for words or symbols:

SPOTLIGHTS

SPOTLIGHTS, just the size you want, can be made with a PAPER STENCIL. Cut a small circle in the center of the paper. By adjusting the lens and moving the paper you can aim the spot of light wherever you want it.

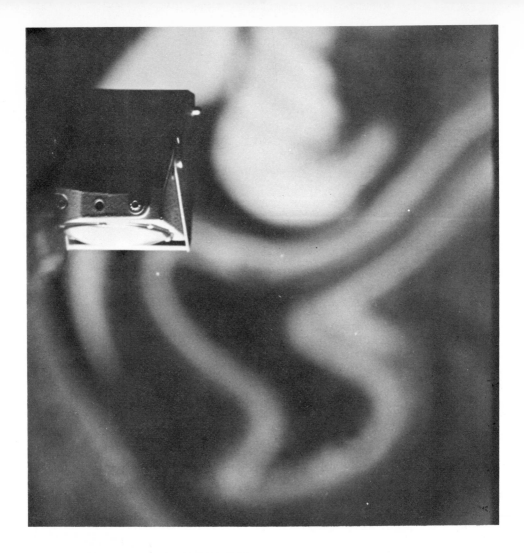

FLUID LIGHT PROJECTION

One of the easiest and most fascinating of the fluid effects is pictured on the page at left. A clear glass bowl containing a little water is moved in a circular rhythmic pattern in the space between the STAGE and the LENS of the overhead. In this projection, a cut-paper stencil is used on the STAGE.

The projected fluid image, as shown above, is a swirl and glow of constantly changing waves of light. The spontaneity and the element of the unexpected intrigue the viewer with lights that dance before the eyes.

You will want to explore the different effects that are possible by moving the water slowly or swiftly. Proficiency in fluids will come with experimentation and practice.

FLUID LIGHTS and SCRIPTURE

In a workshop with Catholic seminarians, four of the students were interested in using fluid lights with scripture. They selected the Gospel account of Jesus meeting the woman at the well. Their thought was that by utilizing an effective light environment, the story would be dramatized and experienced, rather than simply read and listened to.

The students began with the most obvious shape—the well. They cut out a silhouette that looked like a "wishing well" from rural America. But this didn't seem to picture the meaning of the meeting.

What was the important central image in this story? Was it "well" or was it the "water"?

> *"Whoever drinks this water will never thirst again."*

The *water* was the centering image. The students began exploring various fluid environments.

The scripture was finally read dramatically using three voices: Christ, the Samaritan woman and a narrator. A large circle of light projecting through a greenish-blue transparency was dimmed in slowly as the reading began. The projection was slightly out of focus and the bowl of water technique kept the image in ever-so-gentle motion. The projected light fell upon the readers as well as on the wall behind them. The actors, their shadows and the fluid images became one within the context of the story. There was no sense of background or foreground. The people sharing the experience could <u>feel</u> the water. Some commented that they even became a little thirsty.

In later evaluation of the creative process, the students mentioned that their first attempts with the fluid effect were not very satisfying. The movement of the water was too fast and too much of a distraction. Only by slowing down the moving water and controlling it carefully did the projected light become an <u>effective</u> rather than a <u>dominating</u> environment.

FLUID LIGHT and GATHERING

The mosaic of brilliant colors created by the projection of
glass pebbles in water, as pictured on the next two pages,
has been used in a number of different ways. Sometimes as
environment for a dance sequence; sometimes in combination
with other projections to create a joyous outburst of color.

This projection effect was used in an especially meaningful
way in a workshop at Marshall University in West Virginia.

> As a part of the GATHERING, each person was greeted
> at the door with a warm welcome and the gift of a
> small glass shape. On a low table in the center of
> the meeting hall, an overhead was projecting a dish
> of clear water. Each person was invited to put the
> piece of colored glass into the water as he or she
> joined the group seated on the floor. Thus, each
> person became a part of the circle of light on the
> wall. The small children were captivated with the
> idea and gathered closely around the projector. We
> all knew which piece of glass was ours. Later in
> the celebration, colored dye was added to the water.
> The DIMMING TECHNIQUE, as described on page 59, made
> the individual shapes melt and blend.

> The opening meditation helped us sense the individual-
> ity and the combined beauty of each person in this
> group of about two hundred people. One member of the
> workshop, a young girl, had written a song:

> > "One and one are two
> > Two together...two together
> > Then three...then four."

> It was a very singable song with verses that amplified
> the idea of reaching out beyond ourselves to those
> around, waiting to be reached.

> At the closing, the mosaic of color which now repre-
> sented the people more than ever, was projected again
> as a part of a very joyous SCATTERING.

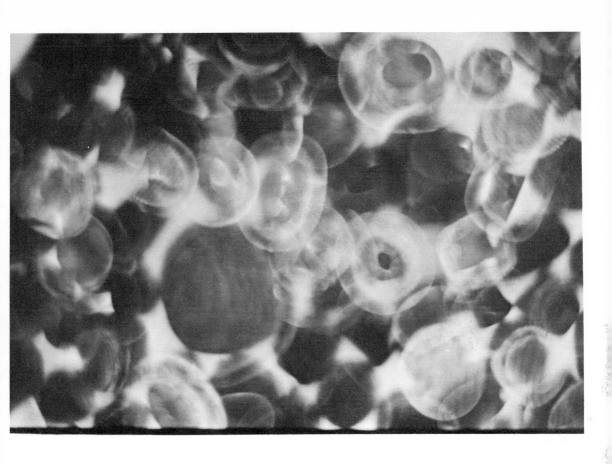

SOFT—FOCUS TECHNIQUE

The picture on the left shows another view of the glass pebbles
and water in a Pyrex pie plate. (Glass pebbles are flattened
transparent marble shapes. They are used in handicraft projects
and can be obtained at art stores.) Also illustrated is the
moving of the FOCUS KNOB on the overhead. A slow, evolving type
of movement happens when a projector is taken in and out of
focus. The picture above shows the glass pebbles projected "out
of focus." This creates a shimmering, jewel-like effect when
seen in color. To maximize the circular effect of both bowl and
glass shapes, the STAGE has been masked with a large paper STENCIL.

An important skill to learn with the overhead is modulation
of light intensity. Images and colors can be dimmed in or out
much like the dissolve effect in films. The picture at the
left demonstrates how it is done. By moving the fingers in
front of the lens, another kind of light motion can be achieved.
As the fingers come closer together they slowly block out the
projected light, darkening the image until it disappears. The
lens becomes hot so it is a good idea to have a soft cloth
handy for long blackouts.

This DIMMING TECHNIQUE should be used for subtle effects and
whenever a transparency needs to be changed. Like stage lighting, the changes should be as imperceptible as possible. It is
this kind of artistry that makes the difference between a dis-
jointed visual presentation and a memorable creation. Harsh
edges of light, shadows of hands, noticeable bowls of water,
etc., distract the viewer from the main thought or mood of the
light expression.

LIGHT SHIELD

The overhead casts a great deal of reflected light in the space
surrounding the projector. When front projection is used, complete blackouts are difficult. One group solved the problem by
designing a temporary cardboard light shield. A large piece of
pliable cardboard was attached to the top of the corner post and
folded down like a hood. A hole was cut so that the lens could
project the image. The area immediately around the STAGE was
kept free and accessible.

FOUR HANDS ARE BETTER THAN TWO!

In order to produce a smooth, artistic *light expression* it is
best to have two people working with each overhead. One person
is responsible for the sequence of transparencies and follows
the script. The second person handles the dimming and fluid
effects. It takes a great deal of teamwork. Timing becomes
crucial. A sense of creative spontaneity combined with organ-
izational ability for a dependable flow of sequences are the
qualities most desirable in a projection team. Usually the team
is a part of a larger team handling the various elements in a
combined effort.

PRISM TECHNIQUE

A PRISM is a transparent glass or plexiglas body that can reflect, refract or disperse light. It is used in optical instruments.

A right-angle PRISM rotated as illustrated in front of the projection lens sends images dividing and reflecting around the room. It is possible to motorize the PRISM, but hand-operated projections are more interesting. The mechanical rotation easily becomes monotonous or mesmerizing. In some *light expressions* this effect may be desired.

The photograph at the right shows an abstract paper-stencil projection being refracted. The same technique can be used with slide or film projectors to fragment and disperse images.

GLASS and PLASTIC 3–DIMENSIONAL SHAPES

A plexiglas salad bowl was used to project this radiant design
as a background for the empty manger in a pre-Christmas Celebration at the Congregational Church in Western Springs, Illinois.
The DIMMING and FOCUSING TECHNIQUES were used to keep the delicate
patterns slowly changing and evolving. Color was added with a
color wheel and other transparencies. At one point in the celebration the screen was filled with news event images.

The overheads and projectionists were hidden from the view of the congregation. A rear-projection screen was set on the steps of the sanctuary. The equipment was placed behind the screen near the altar. (Further explanation of rear-projection and projector placement will be found in a later section of this book.) This arrangement avoided the intrusion of the equipment and unnecessary shadows. The projectionists were very much a part of what was going on, yet they were not a visual distraction to the meditative quality of the service.

FOUND OBJECTS

By using small, newly budding branches on an overhead projector, a workshop group in Naramata, British Columbia, created
a stark and plaintive environment. It was a fitting background for a movement and song expression dealing with the
brutality of war. As people moved within the shadows and
light, it seemed as if a Japanese brush drawing had come to
life.

FOUND OBJECTS of other types can capture the highlights of a
group's experience and thus add symbols of clearly understood
meaning.

> In a celebration at Loyola University, a group of
> priests and nuns wanted to express some of the up-
> tightness they felt when their summer courses began.
> To recall the tensions of their initial struggles
> they projected a six-foot length of plastic hospital
> tubing on an overhead projector. The tubing was
> wadded into a ball and placed on the projector stage.
> The warmth of the light caused the tubing to slowly
> open and untangle. It was an appropriate sign for
> the gradual relaxing of tensions and the opening up
> of people's freedom to be themselves.

COLOR WHEELS

A COLOR WHEEL is a very useful addition to any light sequence.
A complete color wheel consists of three basic parts: the
wheel, the stand and a small motor to provide movement. The
wheel is arranged so that the projector light beam passes
through the color segments of the rotating wheel. A moving
color wheel offers the advantage of continuous, controlled
color change. It can be rotated manually for special effects.

Acrylic discs are available for making unusual color wheels
with transparent projection paint, Cryst-L-Craze or colored
acetate.

The color wheel can be used with slides, films, overhead projections or with a simple spotlight.

PAINT or OIL SWIRLS

For a spectacular color effect use any of the following liquids
for projecting on water:

> Cryst-L-Craze
> Transparent Paints
> Colored Oils

The illustrations on the next two pages show the technique and
result. With your imagination supply color and motion.

Here is the procedure:

> Set a large clock crystal or flat-bottomed clear
> glass dish on the overhead STAGE. Half-fill it
> with water. Gently pour streams of color from
> two or three different bottles on to the surface
> of the water. Actual testing will be your best
> guide as to the quantity of color to use. The
> colors should float on the water filling the
> projection area with swirling color. With an
> ordinary drinking straw, blow evenly from one
> edge of the dish in order to keep the colors
> moving.

Cryst-L-Craze is more easily available that the other types
of color. A note of CAUTION: Cryst-L-Craze has a very strong
vapor. Allow for adequate ventilation. It is also messy to
clean up. Acetone will remove it. The dish should be emptied
carefully. If soaked overnight in water containing a little
vinegar, the paint will float off easily.

This technique projects a beautiful environment for dancers.
In one memorable celebration it was used effectively as a part
of the closing...the SCATTERING. The spiraling colors were
projected from a distance across the ceiling. As the people were
invited to carry the spirit out into the world with them, the
music and colors moved them into action.

There are many other combinations of chemicals, dyes, oils,
with water that create surprising effects. You will want to
try your hand at experimenting. Some of them are too difficult
to control, but they are fun to watch and sometimes spark other
ideas that can be used.

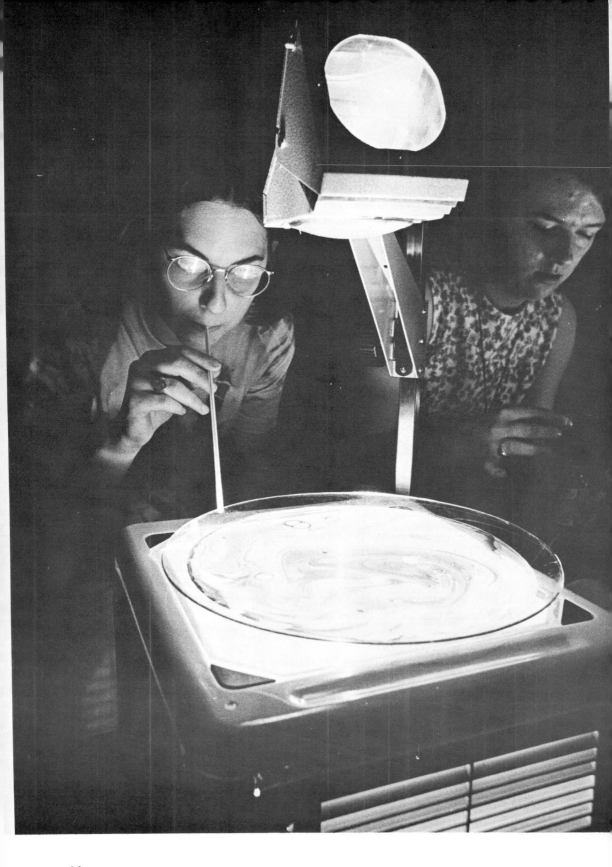

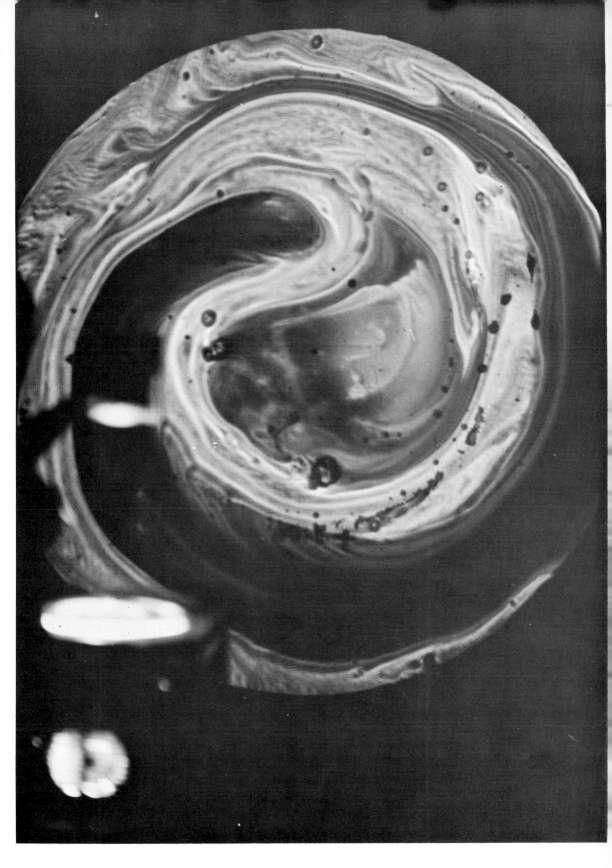

USING TWO or MORE OVERHEADS

When two overhead projectors are used, the possibilities for
unusual effects are multiplied. Beautiful overlays of color
and design, combined with fluid movement, paint a fantasy
environment.

The illustration at the right shows a sea of moving color projected from one overhead using Cryst-L-Craze on water. A
second overhead is projecting plain white star-shapes using a
paper-stencil.

Sometimes one overhead can project a simple background color.
An eleven inch square of rippled or krinkled plexiglas can be
obtained in rich colors and is ideal for these backgrounds.
The use of the DIMMING TECHNIQUE with plexiglas produces a-
mazing results.

SPLASH TECHNIQUE

Imagine the projection pictured on the next page growing and
pulsing before you. The splash of bubbles looks as if it is
coming right out at you—like a surprise bursting open.

To accomplish this effect, two concave clear glass containers
are needed. Large clock crystals, eleven or twelve inches in
diameter are the most satisfactory. One container should be
slightly larger than the other.

Place the larger container on the overhead STAGE. Pour in a
little mineral oil, shampoo or colored glycerin. Then use the
smaller container to squeeze and squash the oil. This movement
is projected as the splashing, organic-like action with circles
of bubbles and foam. Each time you press the top container
down, different patterns emerge and spread out. As you release
the pressure, bringing the top container up, the patterns draw
back together.

The Pablo Light Company, professional light artists, made
dramatic use of this effect as part of their visual interpretation of a Virgil Fox organ concert at the Auditorium Theater in
Chicago. As the powerful rhythms of a Bach fugue filled the
theater, vibrant splashes of color accented the music.

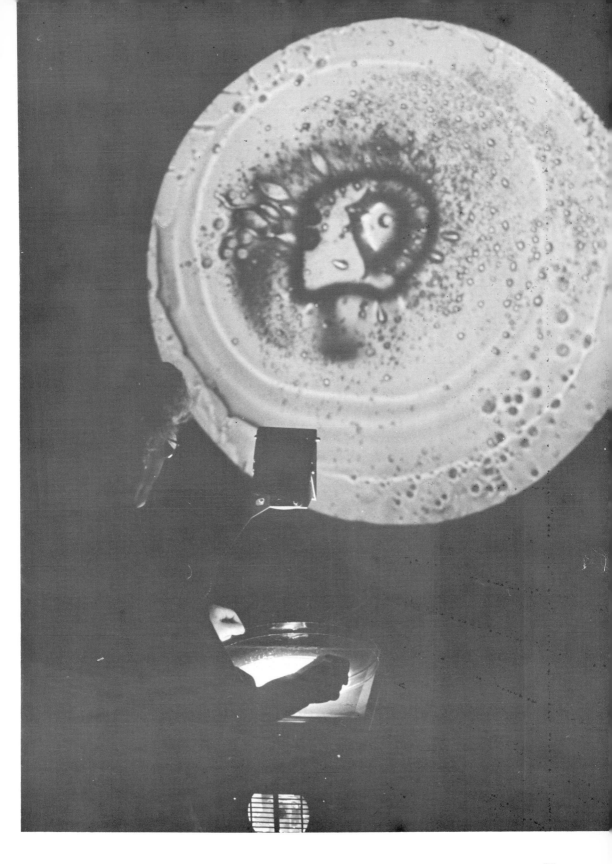

REFINING THE VISUAL IMAGE

In designing for celebration there is a need to constantly revise, reshape, rethink what it is that we do. The same kind of self-criticism is necessary for any artistic discipline. Here are a number of key points to keep in mind when developing the FLUID LIGHT sequence:

>the SPACE involved for projection
>>a stage?
>>a screen?
>>an entire room?

>the POSITION of the projectionists
>>is there enough room for materials and movement?
>>will the projectionists be seen?
>>will light from projecting equipment be in anyone's eyes?

>the TIME allowed for the sequence
>>is there sufficient time for preparation?
>>how much variety in images does the time call for?
>>can transitions, dimming and changes in transparencies be made smoothly?

>the MESSAGE of the media
>>what are the visuals communicating?
>>are they background or foreground?

FLUID LIGHT MOVEMENT usually up-stages whatever else may be happening. The brilliant moving lights are like magnets that draw our eyes to them. It is usually best to slow down the movement or to stop it completely when other media, such as a speaker or singer, are to be emphasized.

THE SHOCKING FACTS ABOUT OVERHEADS

No, this is not a headline from a scandal paper. We are simply advising you to take special precautions when using water with electrical equipment. Be sure to check power lines and extension cords to make sure no wires are exposed. Also, keep all flammable materials away from electrical equipment. No unusual effect is worth the risk of an accident.

Part 4
SLIDE & FILM PROJECTION

THE 35mm PROJECTOR

The 35mm Slide Projector is an essential part of *light expression*. It can be used singly in many creative ways or it can be combined with other lighting effects. Large-scale events might implement as many as six or eight Slide Projectors.

The basic principle of slide projection is the same in all models. The method of <u>changing slides</u> varies immensely.

Know your projector so that you can rely on its performance.

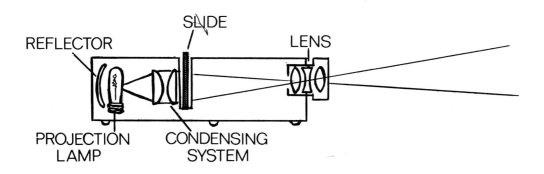

REFLECTOR   SLIDE   LENS

PROJECTION LAMP   CONDENSING SYSTEM

The BASIC PARTS of a SLIDE PROJECTOR

If you plan to purchase new equipment or are able to choose from an audio-visual resource center, look for these advantages in a slide projector:

> A 500 watt Projection Lamp – This will give the necessary brightness for any size gathering.

> Smooth, fast Slide Changer - The loading and handling should be as simple as possible. Quick slide changes with little or no flashes of black or white light in between are important for the smooth flow of the presentation.

Slide Tray - The slide magazine or carousel should
    hold a fairly large number of slides. (Avoid
    the 120 slide carousel. It jams too easily
    and cannot take the hand-made slides.) Carousel
    trays of 60 to 80 slide capacity are preferable.

Quiet Motor - Because of the intense heat from the
    bulb, every projector needs a cooling system.
    Some models have a less noisy fan than others.
    The noise can be a source of annoyance during
    a presentation.

Zoom Lens - Lenses have different focal lengths.
    To state·it simply: at a given distance some
    lenses project a larger image than others. The
    zoom lens is an alternate lens unit that can
    change the magnification of the image. It
    allows you to accommodate the size of the pro-
    jection to the room and to the distance avail-
    able for projecting.

    It is especially useful when more than one slide
    projector is being used. It makes it much easier
    to line up the images.

    The zoom lens can be used as a special effect to
    slowly enlarge or diminish the screen image.

Remote Control Device - This special switch allows
    you the freedom of standing a few feet away
    from the projector or walking around while
    changing slides.

    When using 2 or 3 projectors, the remote control
    switches can be taped in a row or at a convenient
    spot on a table, thus, forming a control panel
    which can be worked with one hand.

2"x 2" PHOTOGRAPHIC SLIDES

A growing slide collection is a valuable
resource for *light expressions*. With the
wide variety of cameras available, it is
not difficult for the average person to
make good color slides. Many of the cameras practically take care of the technical part for you. Excellent books on
photographic technique can easily be
found in bookstores and libraries. (See
the EXPANDING RESOURCES List, p. 138)

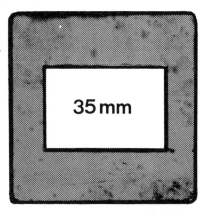

2" X 2" slides come in three types—
illustrated here. All three can be used
in the same projector. The only visual
difference will be the size of the projection.

The 35mm slide is photographed and
developed more inexpensively than the
others. However, the cost of the insta-
matic camera is considerably less.

The Super size slide gives a large
picture area, but the processing is
much more expensive than the other two.

Plastic or cardboard slide mounts can
be obtained in all of these sizes.
Super size slide mounts are the most
practical for creative slide-making
since they offer the largest amount
of space for working.

In choosing sizes, consideration
should be given to the way in which
the slides will be shown. Double or
triple screen projection should have
uniformly-sized slides if the wide,
cineramic effect is desired. Slides
in a series can be of alternating
sizes, but it is necessary to be
aware of the staccato movement the
flashing images will make.

MAKING SLIDES PHOTOGRAPHICALLY

POSSIBILITIES FOR SEEING WITH A CAMERA

Each day
　　　　a collage of moments
　　　　　　　　　encounters
　　　　　　　　　times of success
　　　　　　　　　times of disappointment

　　　　not so neatly arranged in a list
　　　　but newly woven into the ever-growing network
　　　　　　　　called HUMAN PERSON.

　　　　And in these fleeing moments
　　　　I wonder how much I miss.

The style of photography that enables celebration is one that focuses upon the <u>meaning of the instant</u>. The photographer's eye sensitively selects out from the day's collage of events, a moment when the collage coalesces into a microcosm—and the wholeness of the world converges in the revelation of a moment. The photographic image retains this moment, offering the time needed to savor it and penetrate it for meanings.

How can we make pictures that compel attention?

The photography of celebration requires sensitivity. The person behind the lens must discover how to let things and people reveal themselves. The key idea is "make" the picture, rather than "take" it.

　　　　"making" implies a dialogue, a construction, a cooperating conversation between the photographer and that which is photographed.

　　　　"taking" implies a sneak shot, something done alone without the full knowledge of the other party. This is characteristic of the tourist's shot where the picture tells that "we were here and went there".

The photography of celebration will have the quality of awakening the imagination and opening the mind to a realization that there is more to understanding life.

> A memorable photograph was of a young boy walking very fast. The picture showed the boy in full stride with both feet off the ground, as if he were suspended in mid-air.
>
> The photographer "caught the person in the act" of being himself. There was nothing artificial or posed about the action. It was the kind of picture that prompted thoughts like: "In my hurriedness I, too, must often lose touch with the ground. Instead of progressing forward, I seem to be thrashing the air, going nowhere."

The photography of celebration is a revealing art of the instant.

> A member of The Center made two pictures of an old man sitting on a park bench. The first picture was "taken" from a distance. The picture was not particularly compelling.
>
> A <u>distant instant</u> is rarely the kind of dialogue that awakens meanings in the viewer. Close visual contact is usually necessary for personal involvement.
>
> The second picture was "made", in conversation with the elderly gentleman. When the photographer asked him if he could make a picture, the old man straightened up, fixed his tie and hat and said, "O.K., I"m ready."
>
> The photographer saw a fresh breath of life coming to the old man simply because someone showed an interest in him as a person. "It was something of a 'resurrection' event for the old man," he desribed, "and that quality came through in the photograph."

Like every art form, a certain amount of technique must be acquired. Much depends upon your ability to SEE and to FEEL into a situation.

Here are some ideas which might help you, or groups with whom you are working, to make photographic slides that have a depth of meaning, as well as good composition:

1. Use a FRAMER to take a look at the world around you. FRAMING is a useful technique for sharpening visual awareness to patterns of dark and light, color and texture. Use a slide mount or cut a small rectangular window in a piece of cardboard. Viewing life through the small frame is similar to using the viewfinder of the camera. The discipline of confining the field of vision to the boundaries of the frame trains the eye to look more closely at deatails and relationships of contrast.

When you look through a framer several significant things happen:

You edit out the whole of the life picture, concentrating on that small portion which interests you.

You look through one eye, thus losing some depth of field.

You feel a need to make order and sense out of the things caught within the frame—disregarding the total picture.

If you are "framing" people, you realize how hard it is to follow them in motion. You notice how self-conscious they become under observation.

If you are in a group and others are "framing" you, it may help you sense the feelings of the person being photographed.

2. Photograph things and people within your own experience.
   Get to know your subject before aiming the camera. It is
   very evident when a photographer has rapport with his subject. There is some kind of dialogue going on. The picture has drawing power because the photographer is saying,
   "This matters to me. These are my friends."

> There is real contact with the three faces
> grinning at us from the top of the page. We
> share some fun-secret. It is hard not to respond.

3. Document the touch of the human. Look for places where man
   is leaving his mark on the world—on other human beings.

4. Document moments of wonder—of quiet thought. Search out the human cry. Capture the split second when something is happening—

> the breath of a small child at the instant when the air strikes the candles on the birthday cake.

5. Get in close on the subject. Many a bird has been lost in the bush because the camera was twenty feet away. Sharpen your eye for the contrasts of shadow and sunshine. Without the bright patches of sunlight and the deep shadow areas, the little girl in the picture below would disappear into the wild phlox and never be seen.

6. Group photography offers another kind of experience in
   seeing. When the photographs are developed and shared
   there is the added dimension of remembering what the
   original moment felt and looked like.

   As part of a Sunday morning celebration class in Villa
   Park, Illinois, a group of children were sent out with
   cameras to explore the neighborhood for signs of life.
   On a previous Sunday, in preparation for the actual
   photographing, the children had experimented with the
   FRAMING technique, studied textures and shadows, and
   made Contact Paper Slides. They were anxious to begin
   with the camera.

   The photographic expedition was limited to the actual
   class time, but the children used every minute to discover the bright, new world within their familiar land-
   scape. The boy who made this photograph of a tree was
   amazed at the result. He had been fascinated by the
   light shining through the leaves and by the up-reach
   of branches. He thought he was focusing on a squirrel
   climbing a high branch; instead, he captured the very
   growth of the tree.

PHOTOGRAMS are an excellent introduction to the process of photographic development. They are made by placing several items on photographic paper, exposing the paper to light for 10-20 seconds and then developing the paper in the same way as a photographic print. The light-sensitive paper must be handled in the dark. Any small room without windows can be converted temporarily into a darkroom. A source of running water is needed for washing the prints.

The PHOTOGRAM above was made by placing five forks on the paper. The lightest areas are places where the forks completely touched the light-sensitive paper, blocking out the direct light. Flat objects create solid white silhouettes. Transparent materials let enough light through to print varying shades and textures.

This technique has been used in workshops as a group activity in new ways of sensing. People enjoy sharing the surprise configurations made by their objects. Mounted PHOTOGRAMS make a fine exhibition.

PAINTING SLIDES

Fascinating abstract slides can be made with various types of
transparent paints and a little ingenuity. The Cryst-L-Craze
paint is the easiest to use and it's always full of surprises.
When it dries it forms a tracery of lovely organic patterns
which project in brilliant array. This paint was developed to
decorate the backs of fish aquariums and other glass decorations
through which light would pass. Glass stain is used for painting
on glass. Transparent Projection Paint is made especially for
use on acetate. These paints can be used alone or in combination
on acetate transparencies. They all have a strong vapor and are
flammable. Care should be taken to find a room with adequate
ventilation for working and for the drying process. Extra pre-
caution should be taken in handling the paints. Since they are
designed to be permanent on glass, they are very difficult to
remove from clothing.

MATERIALS:

> Transparent acetate (hard surface, medium weight
>   .010 inch thick) cut to fit exactly within the
>   slide mount
> Slide Mounts (Super or 35mm size)
> Cryst-L-Craze in various colors
> Glass Stain or Transparent Projection Paint
> Toothpicks and cardboard sticks
> Newspaper and waxed paper
> White scrap paper

PROCESS:

1. Cover the work area with newspaper. Work on the
    acetate square over white paper so that you can
    see what you are doing.

    Use small sticks or 1/8 inch strips of cardboard
    instead of brushes to apply paint. Let the paint
    flow from the stick onto the acetate. It takes
    only a few drops to cover a slide.

Let the colors run into each other.
Exciting things happen when they
mix and over-lap. Try dropping
one color on top of another.
Spread the paint out to the edges
of the slide. Usually a richer
effect is achieved if the entire
area is covered with color.

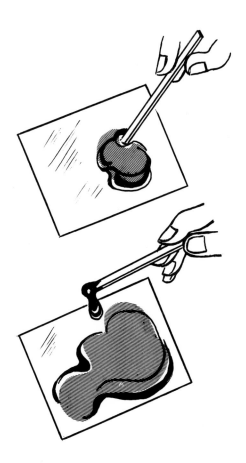

Avoid mixing too many colors.
Muddy browns result from over-
working the slide.

Experiment with different
techniques:

> dripping, dabbing, blotting,
>   blowing, swirling,
>
> applying a second layer
>   after the first one dries,
>
> scratching into a partly
>   dry slide,
>
> adding granules of sugar
>   or salt.

Texture can be developed by
combining bits of weeds, threads
or small pieces of acetate with the
paint colors on the slide. The
paint will act as a glue as well as
a color surface.

A related series of abstract slides
for two or three screen projection
can be made by painting on a long
strip of acetate and cutting the
individual slide shapes after the
paint dries.

Cryst-L-Craze and Glass Stain have different bases and they dry at a different rate. The Cryst-L-Craze paint will crystallize slowly from the outside edges in, as it dries. The Glass Stain will remain the way you apply it. The two can be used together for unusual effects.

OVERHEAD TRANSPARENCIES can be made in the very same ways as the small slides. You can also apply a thick layer of paint to an eleven inch square of acetate and then cover it with another square of the same size, sandwiching the color in between. When it dries, the projected transparency has intense color and a three-dimensional depth.

2. Place the finished slides on waxed paper to dry. Let them dry thoroughly. It takes about two hours in a dry climate. It may take over-night depending on the humidity.

3. Mount the slide carefully. It will jam in the projector if any small edges stick out or if the slide becomes bent. These slides become permanent.

The OVERHEAD TRANSPARENCIES can be mounted with a binding of masking tape around all four edges.

SLIDE-MAKING has been an enjoyable part of many of our workshops.
People find themselves intrigued with the mixing of colors. The
process is simple, yet there is endless opportunity for innovation.
They discover that they are more creative than they once thought,
and that they can be expressive in an abstract way.

After the fun of making the slides, what do you do with them?
How do you experience them?
How do they become a part of celebration?

It takes artistry of another kind to weave the slides into meaning and "event". A shared response to the spectacular shapes
and colors can take many forms. There is something so vibrant--
so alive about the colors that they invite participation.

A group of people in Springfield, Massachusetts wrote HAIKU or
three-line poems about their own particular slide. These were
read as the slides were projected.

> Light burst, Sun burst
>   Cut with silver paths
> Leading where, I wonder?

> Thistle-down shards
>   Bursting forth
>   implosively.

Sometimes the projected slides have been used to create an
opening environment. Sometimes one or two slides have been used
as a focal point for a meditation.

A beautiful instrumental improvisation was played with each
musician interpreting a different color on a projected slide.
Each instruemnt took on the mood and shape of the color in sound.

Projected Cryst-L-Craze slides make a stunning background for
dancers, who in turn, add a new dimension of shadow and movement
to the visual image.

In a programmed photographic slide sequence, the abstract color
slides make delightful intervals of change. Since they depend
almost entirely upon color for their impact, they tend to lift
spirits and affirm life. They symbolize new forms and possibilities and yet are closely related to the organic patterns of
nature from the microscopic world to the outer universe.

CONTACT PAPER SLIDES

The CONTACT PAPER METHOD of slide-making is a quick, simple and economical way to put immediacy and group involvement into multi-media events. Groups can make and use the slides in the same day. Transparent CONTACT PAPER can be purchased in most hardware departments.

MATERIALS:

> Transparent CONTACT PAPER cut into 2 inch squares (this allows extra space on the edges for handling)
> Clear acetate (medium weight #.010) cut to fit exactly within the slide mount.
> Cardboard or plastic slide mounts (Super size is preferable)
> Bowl for hot water
> Scissors
> Magazines with slick surface paper, such as: "Time"—"Life"—etc.
> Paper towels

PROCESS:

> 1. With a slide mount, frame the portion of a magazine page you wish to use. Study the compositional elements within the frame. Look for strong contrast in black and white or in color.

2. Peel the backing from a square of CONTACT PAPER. Handle it carefully by the edges. Fingerprints will show in the final projection. Place the adhesive side on the selected area of the magazine page and smooth gently to avoid air bubbles.

Find a hard, smooth table or floor surface to work on. Use a few pieces of paper for padding under the square.

Thoroughly rub the entire surface with the round of your fingernail or with a smooth-edged tool, like the bowl of a spoon, until the milky look completely disappears and the ink becomes a part of the adhesive. When rubbing, exert heavy pressure, but avoid warping or scratching the surface.

3. Cut out the square, allowing extra margin for handling. Place the square in a bowl of hot water and let it soak for a few minutes. The hotter the water, the quicker the soaking process. The paper backing will slip off easily leaving the print image in the CONTACT PAPER. Paper and print qualities vary in different magazines. Some require longer soaking than others. Any paper residue on the transparency can be removed by returning the contact print to the hot water and rubbing the surface gently. When working with large groups, change the water frequently.

4. Place the square of contact transparency on a paper towel to dry, ADHESIVE SIDE UP. Allow it to dry thoroughly.

5. When dry, cover the adhesive side of the square with clear acetate to protect and strengthen the transparency.

The contact square usually retains enough adhesiveness to form a good weld. Smooth it with your fingers. The warmth of your hands aids the process. Trim all the edges carefully so that the slide can be slipped into the mount for projection. No edges should be allowed to bulge or hang out because they will cause the projector to jam.

CONTACT PAPER SLIDES project
with a dot separation quality
that tends to communicate the
"nowness" of the daily papers. Pictures with strong dark-light
contrast make the clearest projections. Full-color pictures
have the tactile quality of impressionistic paintings or the TV
screen. The effect is quite different from that of photographic
slides.

Experiment with different types of magazines. Some transfer an
image with more clarity than others.

Pictures and words can be combined in a collage arrangement. Lay
the various small pieces in the way they are to appear when projected. Place a square of CONTACT PAPER over the composition,
then rub briskly. The slide pictured above on the right was made
in this way.

Large transparencies for the overhead projector can be made in
the same way. It takes a lot of rubbing on the larger area, but
the advantage of being able to cover a whole wall or ceiling with
current happenings makes up for all the work.

The words projected into a fluid light background in this
illustration were typed on regular mimeograph stencil paper
and mounted in a 35mm slide mount.

To make MIMEO SLIDES:
>   Use a slide mount to line up the size of the opening.
>   Type the words on the stencil just as you would for
>   mimeographing.
>   Cut out the rectangle with some extra margin.
>   Cut an identical shape of thin protective acetate
>   and slip the two pieces carefully into the slide mount.
>   The slide is then ready for projection.

WORDS AND PHRASES can be written on clear acetate slides with
fineline marking pens, India ink and pens, or wax pencils.
Write-On Slides can be purchased at camera stores, but it is
more economical to make your own. Use clear matte acetate in
the slide mounts. It is transparent, but frosted on one side
to facilitate writing. Even pencil lines will show up clearly.

CREATING WITH POLARIZED LIGHT

The phenomenon of light polarization can be used to bring movement into slide projections. By means of polarizing filters and
specially made slides, the screen becomes alive with changing
color and shapes.

EQUIPMENT and MATERIALS:

        Slide projector
        Polarizing wheel placed in front of lens
          (the spinner should be motorized for best effect)
        Polarizing filter
        Slides made with bi-refringent material

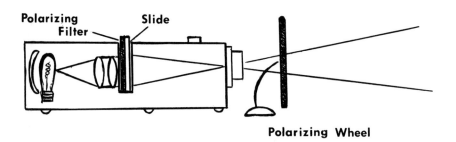

MAKING POLARIZING SLIDES

MATERIALS:

  Polarizing filters (you will need two. One should be the
    2 inch square size of the slide. The other should be
    the wheel or a larger piece of polarizing material to be
    moved by hand.)
  Thin glass cover slides (2" X 2")
    Thick acetate may be used.
    The polarizing filter itself may be used.
  Cellophane tape
  Scraps of colored acetate or cellophane
  Pieces of mylar and polyethylene
      (Photo motion material can be purchased from
      science stores. It is self-adhesive material that
      can be cut into designs and applied to transparencies.)

The cellophane, mylar and polyethylene are called "bi-refringent material". They refract or bend the light ray as it passes through. The linear polarizing filters cut out various color-producing light waves, allowing others to pass through and reflect. As one of the polarizing filters is turned, different light waves are being cut out, so the colors in each section are constantly changing. This produces the kaleidescopic effect.

PROCESS:

> First, experiment a little with the effect of light polarization. Crumple a cellophane wrapper. Place it between two polarizing filter squares and hold it up to the light. You will see colors that were not originally there. Now try moving one of the filters. The colors change with each slight rotation.

To begin making slides, take a piece of glass cover slide or a square of polarizing filter and stretch cellophane tape in criss-cross or crazy quilt patterns, layer upon layer, around it. If the glass is used, you will need to add the polarizing filter when you project it. The filter can be slipped in with the slide or, in some projectors, inserted in front of the condensing lens.

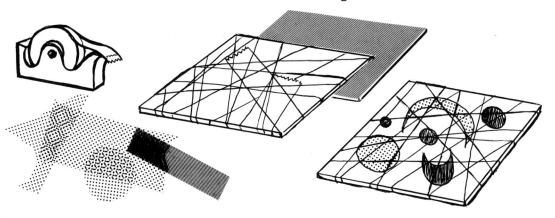

After making a few slides and experimenting with them, you will notice that color is determined by the number of layers of bi-refringent material, the tension in the tape as you apply it, and the other types of materials you might add.

Try taping cellophane to the filter. Explore the effects produced by mylar or polyethylene wrappers. Add a drop of mineral oil between layers. Add bits of thread or shapes cut from colored acetate. You can draw with India ink or felt markers on the tape-wrapped slides. Press-type letters can be applied for words.

Using these same techniques, you can make transparencies for an OVERHEAD projector. You will need a large polarizing spinner which should be attached immediately under or in front of the lens.

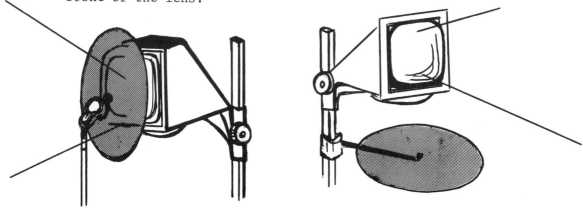

The motorized spinner apparatus that is used for the polarizing wheel can also be used for a color wheel or special effect wheel. You can make these by purchasing plastic transparent discs and adding your own colors in any way you choose. An interesting distortion effect can be achieved by heating an acrylic or plexiglas disc in the oven and bending or rippling it. When used on the spinner with some kind of transparancy or slide, the screen undulates with misty, amorphus shapes.

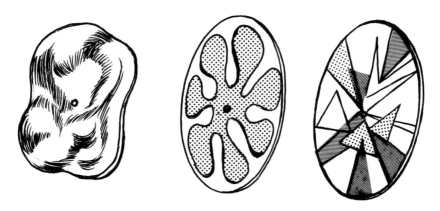

SLIDES ARE FOR SHARING NOT SHOWING

Once the techniques for slide making have been learned, it is most important to develop ways in which the slides can be shared. Too often effective slide images become ineffective when they are shown without imagination or dramatic timing.

Too often people merely show slides.

> In a recent workshop with college students, a group of the participants programmed slides for three projectors and a tape recorder. The images were photographs from current magazines and the music was short excerpts from popular hits. The piece lasted 45 minutes.
>
> There were a few memorable moments, but not e-nough to keep everyone's attention at a high level. When the piece concluded, the students offered their appraisals:

> > "It was good. It needed editing."
> >
> > "This was much too long. You could have used fewer slides and still made your point."
> >
> > "The pictures were all very familiar. I kept hoping to see something new."
> >
> > "The slides never 'came off the screen' for me. I was a spectator not a partici-pant."
> >
> > "The musical excerpts were too short and choppy. You didn't give me enough time to get into the slides and music."

Editing is essential for effective slide use.

When we design celebrations, we always have more slides than we can use. We have learned that people can quickly reach a saturation point with slides unless the timing is changed and the images present a varied pattern for thought.

Try to communicate in the most basic and clearest way possible.
Use only the essential slides and sounds to make your initial
statement. You can become more elaborate after your basic idea
is made. Doing this will take patience and discipline, but the
art of editing is one worth appropriating.

MASKING

There is something about the continuous squared-ness of slides
that quickly tires the eyes. MASKING is an editing technique
that enables you to focus the viewer's eyes on parts of the
slide. Using opaque paper try MASKING some slides with the
following frame shapes:

BLANK SLIDES are a form of MASKING using opaque materials,
such as construction paper, to completely block out the light
from the projector. BLANK SLIDES are used whenever you want
the screen darkened without having to turn off the projector.
BLANK SLIDES should be used at the very beginning and the end
of a slide presentation to avoid the annoying "white flash" on
the screen which breaks the mood and meaning.

The main focus of visuals is <u>communicating with people</u>.

Communication depends on

- the person (or medium) that is communicating
- the person(s) to whom the message is spoken
- the meaning of the message for the listener
- the style of communication
- the time and place in history

If we lose sight of any of these elements or if we concentrate on only a few and exclude other elements, the chances of a communication break-through are reduced.

Sometimes in planning visuals for celebration, people get all caught up in the technical aspects of slide arranging, or in the "thrill of controlling projectors", and forget about communicating personally with people.

A young minister, who was well versed in audio-visual techniques, and his youth group designed a service. It was programed for six slide projectors, two film projectors and a tape recorder.

The service lacked a sense of "personal presence and warmth."

Everything was projected and all voices were pre-recorded. The hymns were accompanied by beautifully synthesized electronic music. But the congregation didn't sing. People were so fascinated by this new sound that they only listened. The only singing voice was that of the minister's, who was singing from behind a battery of projectors. The noise from the fans on the machines prevented the man from hearing the people.

<u>Don't lose sight of the people</u> when you use projected images.

Keep asking yourself:

"What meaning will this have for the people?"
"Where are the people going to be able to participate?"

Because modern living brings to us a multitude of images, we find that by using more than one slide projector we are able to enable an awareness of the wide scope of fast-moving event which characterizes our world.

By using one, two and three projected images a variety of communicative styles become available to us.

ONE PROJECTED IMAGE

> The single image presents a documentary and linear style.
>
> It characterizes a reporting of events, the stages in the journey, a step-by-step progression.
>
> This style should be used sparingly for dramatic effect.
>
> The single image is often used as a part of the prelude for celebration. It is a simple opening and can effectively center the people's attention on the main idea. The single image is usually a place from which adults and young people can make a common beginning in the visual experience.

TWO PROJECTED IMAGES

With two slide projectors there is the possibility of "dialogue" with contrasts, comparisons and visual simile and metaphor.

On the next page is an example of two different images which are similar in composition. Look at both images. Then cover one of the images and view the other. Now reverse the procedure. What is communicated when the images are seen individually? What is communicated when the pictures are seen together?

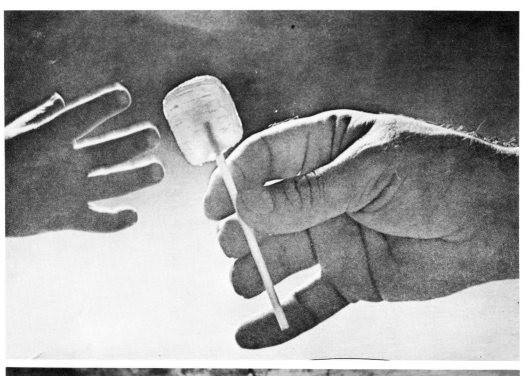

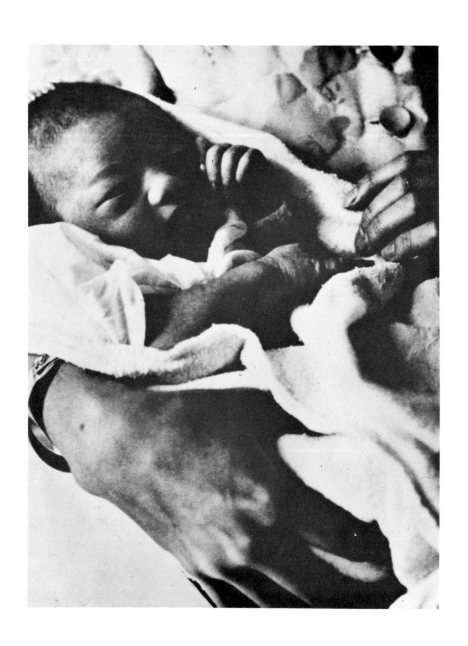

The juxtapositioning of contrasting images will often set up
a totally new feeling, sometimes called a "third effect". This
effect is created by placing seemingly unrelated images in a
visual field with one another. The tensions presented challenge
the viewer's imagination to build a story that links the two
images. This is a very good way to involve the viewer in the
meaning of the visual environment.

THREE PROJECTED IMAGES

Three images offer greater opportunity for inter-play of contrast-comparison. While expanding and broadening our viewpoint, three images enable us to experience the time sequence of past-present-future.

If a series of three images is planned, try to vary the speed at which they are shown and the order in which they appear. Don't always go: "Left-Center-Right" when you change images. Also you might want to explore projecting images vertically instead of always horizontally.

Sometimes you will want to use more than three images at a time. However, this has a <u>mind bombarding</u> effect on the viewer and will soon dull the senses. People seem to be able to comprehend a maximum of five images simultaneously.

103

FILM--A MEDIUM OF MOVEMENT

Unlike the photograph or slide which can freeze the moment,
film presents hundreds of individual photographs in a continuous flow, thus producing the illusion of movement. With this
added dimension, filmic expression gives the time elements of
past-present-future.

Film is a <u>confluence of the senses</u>—a medium meeting place
for the visual, aural, kinesthetic, spacial and temporal. It
is an art that embodies much of the flowing quality so essential to celebration. When used in communal celebration, the
film has the character of being "larger than life". Screen
reality offers us either a close-up perspective or a broader
global awareness of what is going on in the world.

Film-making has become the work of the people. Once the ex-
clusive (and expensive) activity of Hollywood people, films
are now being created by adults, young people and children.
Many high schools and grammar schools use film as a valuable
tool in teaching. College students create films instead of
writing the usual term papers.

With the impact of technological visual languages all of us
have been jolted from a comfortable word-world to the uncer-
tain image-world. The printed word is under suspicion and its
continuing proiority as the only means of communication is
highly questioned. "Viewing" has replaced "reading" as a pri-
mary information source. Data no longer needs to be stored in
massive volumes for now, through filmic storage, the entire
Bible can be contained on celluloid the size of a pin head.

THE FILM IN CELEBRATION

Films used in celebration have more in common with the filmic
styles of "underground film makers" than with commercial theater films. These experimental films have a freshness of dis-
covery and exploration. They are a medium of expression unique
in themselves.

Most of the films we have used in communal celebrations were
created by Robert Wells with Super 8mm equipment. The advantages in using this film format are: it is less expensive than
16mm, it gives a larger image than regular 8mm making the job
of editing easier, and the necessary equipment is lightweight
and compact. Recent advances in Super 8mm cameras and its
greater availability make the filmic process an exciting and
adventuresome one.

The films we have made and used in celebration include:

> Documentary, Montage, Animated, Meditative, T.V.
> commercials and news clips, and Discussion Films.

THE DOCUMENTARY FILM

Celebration grows from experience, not from themes. By filming
an experience we are able to present to the gathered community
the actual visual and acoustical events as they happened.

Two memorable documents which grew from The Center's activities
were THE CROSS WALK and WOBBLES THE CLOWN.

> THE CROSS WALK was filmed during Holy Week to probe
> the question, "What meaning does a cross have in the
> midst of daily life?" The film caught people's re-
> sponses to seeing a 100 pound telephone pole being
> carried along a downtown street during lunch hour.
> The majority of Chicagoans stared, some made jokes or
> sarcastic comments. However, 14 people helped carry
> the pole during the week. They ranged in age from
> teens to adults, students and business people.
>
> The film was used each night in a crucifixion celebra-
> tion at a point when the same telephone pole was
> carried through the center aisle of the church and
> nailed into place near the altar.
>
> WOBBLES THE CLOWN was filmed during Christmas in the
> city. Sister Adelaide, dressed as Wobbles, went into
> downtown shopping crowds asking: "Where is Love in the
> world?" We were probing how deeply commercialism had
> infiltrated the consciousness of people and whether
> Love was only a seasonal event.

Wobbles asked shoppers, children, police, store clerks, and even bus riders. She was invited to homes, office parties and bus tours. There was little fear of the clown. Then Wobbles went to see Santa Claus.

Wobbles: "Hello Santa. Where do you find love in the world?"

Santa: "I don't know, honey. I don't think it exists. That's a word we've just made up. No one loves me and I really don't love anybody."

These films became probes into what people wer thinking and what was going on in our culture, particularly concerning the religious dimension

The Documentary film presents the experience and serves only
as a background image for an "in-person" reporting as part of
the celebration. By having the person present who has had the
experience just seen, we get the "insider's" viewpoint of what
it was like to be there.

THE MONTAGE FILM

> montage: the process of producing a rapid
> sequence of very short scenes to
> show a rapid succession of associ-
> ated ideas or mental images.

Film can picture a multitude of images before our eyes, almost
to the point of overwhelming the senses. The general public
became aware of the technique of showing many images in rapid
succession when the Smothers Brothers aired AMERICAN TIME CAP-
SULE, a three minute film tracing American history from its
beginning to the present.

TAKE A LOOK AT WHAT'S HAPPENING was created in rapid-image style
for The Center's 1969 celebration of world-wide communion. The
film focused our awareness on the global village we live in by
using more than 1,000 pictures from national magazines.

The film is a five minute montage, with some images remaining on
the screen for as long as two seconds and other images staying
on as little as 1/24 of a second. The film was made in an after-
noon and required no splicing. The editing was done with the
camera. Using a tripod and a camera equipped with a single-frame
release button (which allows the film maker to shot one frame at
a time) the pictures passed below the camera's eye. Depending on
the length of viewing time desired, a picture would receive one
or more frames of film.

THE MEDITATIVE FILM

This style of film expression is a focusing of the person's attention, a letting go of distractions and a centering of life
energies towards a single idea. In a quiet restfulness, we are
able to take a concentrated look at those things which often
pass by unnoticed.

The Center created a meditative film for a celebration at
The Ecumenical Witness For Peace (January, 1972). The film,
LIKE CLAY IN THE POTTER'S HANDS, is a close-up view of a potter centering clay on the wheel and forming it into a pot.
This film is based on Jeremiah 18 which speaks of God as
being like the potter with the power to break or build. The
film is available from The Center.

THE ANIMATED FILM

Though the animated film requires art lay-out and patience in
shooting, the effect of an original animation in a celebration
provides some necessary components: humor and surprise.

> In a celebration we were considering how machines
> both enable and enslave humanity. Through a series
> of short films we explored the meaning and growth of
> machines. One of these was an animation of cave
> people.

> The scene went like this: one cave man, who had just
> discovered the wheel, was having trouble getting his
> wheel started. He asked another cave character:
> "Could you jump me?" The cave character leaped high
> over our hero who went chugging down the path deter-
> mined to trade his wheel in for a newer model.

The film took many hours to shoot because of
the changes in movement and the many hours to
edit to synchronize speaking and mouth movements.

THE T.V. COMMERCIAL

Some of the best and most entertaining film work is done in
the one minute television commercial spot. Quite often you
will see a commercial that could be used in a religious celebration. Use your power to borrow and call the station or
write the public relations department of the advertizer. You
can usually obtain the film if you explain what it is you want
to use it for.

Also, news stations will sometimes give you their "out-takes",
pieces of film which they could not air.

For a communion service we used a commercial
bread film during the breaking of bread. The
sound was turned off so that the celebrant's
voice could be heard.

The celebration on machines featured a HERTZ
RENT A CAR film with Don Adams encouraging the
Wright brothers not to give up flying after one
their early attempts failed.

"Give man his wings," cried Adams.

Orville responds as he limps away from the wreck:
"If man wants his wings, let him buy a parakeet!"

THE FILM FOR DISCUSSION

Films will often arouse viewers so much that the people want
to talk about its meaning. THE PARABLE, THE CARPENTER and
A TIME FOR BURNING are a few of the films that churches use
for discussion. A more extensive list will be found in the
back of this book.

It is important to select films that will have meaning for the community viewing them. We have known too many situations where the minister will show a film simply for the sake of showing a film. Or the film will be used to take the place of the sermon.

> A priest showed the excellent film THE EUCHARIST as part of a morning Mass. However, he failed to set the right environment for seeing. As a result the film was a source of irritation rather than inspiration. It was too long for the brief time the community had together and it didn't speak to the mood of the moment. This is not a criticism of the film but rather an illustration of the poor use of a good film.

With long films, we have found it useful to select parts for viewing. This requires that someone see the film ahead of time and make the selection.

When a film is shared the proper environment should be established so that the story line can be received by the people. "Proper environment" means that everything is set-up and organized. The projector is focused and "on cue". Only a simple flip of the switch is needed to start.

Another important part of the "proper environment" is the setting of mood or background. The film should be an integral part of the whole expression, not an intrusion.

PROJECTING SURFACES and SET-UPS

What we project on is as important as what we project. The
types of screen, the way we place the screen and the bright-
ness or dimness of the images all affect the communicative
impact of the visual.

A variety of screen set-ups are possible:

> Front-projection— the viewer and the projectors are
> on the same side of the screen. This set-up is used
> in most theaters with the projecting equipment in a
> booth above the audience. Without a booth, however,
> this style makes people conscious of the equipment
> and distracts from the visual.

> Rear-projection— the projectors are on one side of
> the screen and the viewer is on the other side. This
> allows the equipment and projectionists to remain hid-
> den. Images that are rear-projected will appear in
> reverse when viewed on the screen. To correct this
> slides will be inserted backwards and film will be
> focused into a mirror. The mirror image will then be
> projected.

> Environmental-projection— utilizing the givens of the
> space, the images are focused on buildings, walls,
> ceilings and floors.

> > At a workshop the young people hung a nylon
> > parachute like a tent inside the church and
> > projected on it from the inside and the out-
> > side.

> > In a summer workshop at Loyola University songs
> > were projected on two weather balloons. As the
> > songs finished, the balloons were cut loose and
> > rose like rockets into the night air.

> Mobile-projection— uses screens which are quickly
> moved around. Projectors can be carried about to
> follow the screens. Mobile screens offer the possi-
> bility of changing the viewing surface in an instant.
> These screens permit dancers and actors to weave in
> and through the visuals.

SCREEN SET-UPS

The FLAT screen is a most common visual experience. However, we should be aware of other alternative screen arrangements. Two simple designs are pictured below.

> At the United Presbyterian's Commission on Ecumenical Mission and Relations (August, 1972) a large white wall was provided for projections. We added two nine by nine foot screens on either side of the wall and expanded the viewing surface.

CONCAVE screen with front projecting

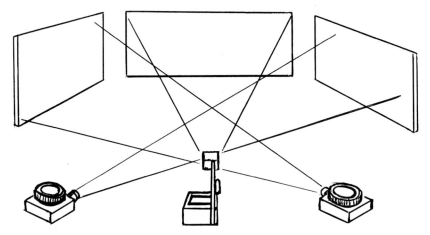

MULTI-LAYERED screen with front and rear projecting allows the people to move through the environment. The keystone shape of the slides on the back wall is created by the angle of projection.

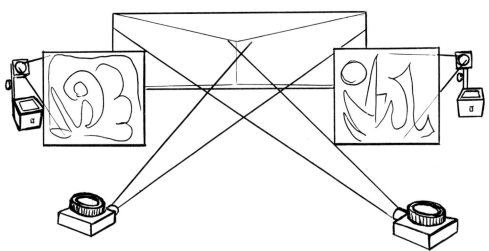

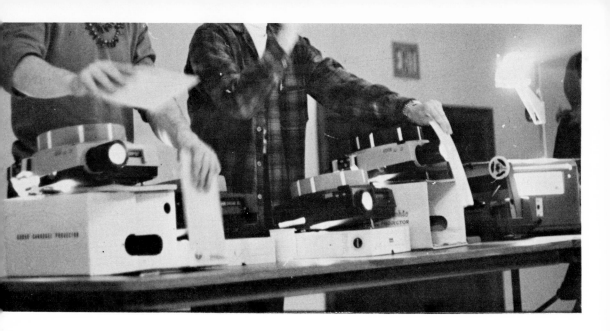

EQUIPMENT SET-UPS

Pictured above is a typical arrangement for film and slide
projectors and overheads. The projectionists are using a
DISSOLVING technique with opaque cards being flashed in
front of two projectors thus preventing the images from ap-
pearing on the screen. The other two projectors are shooting
images on the screen. By changing the cards from projector to
projector the images seem to dissolve into one another rather
than simply flashing off and on.

Often we will need to get projectors above the heads of the
people so that shadows will not appear on the screen. A simple
way of doing this is to build a platform by placing tables on
top of one another as shown below.

REMOTE CONTROL SWITCHES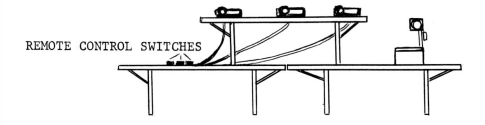

The REMOTE CONTROL SWITCHES can be conveniently taped in one
spot to make a control panel.

Be sure to secure all electrical lines running to the projecting area. If you have your power lines on the floor where the
people are likely to walk or sit, tape the cords to the floor
to avoid anyone tripping or pulling out your power source.

SCREEN FRAMES

We make inexpensive screens from aluminum extrusions which
permit an endless variety of shapes and sizes. By using
nine foot lengths to construct the projecting panels and
aluminum legs of various lengths, we have constructed simple
nine by nine foot screens or complex, four-sided screens,
each side being nine by twenty-seven feet. This latter
screen is pictured on page 133 as it was used in a Communion
Celebration at the General Synod meeting of the United Church
of Christ (June, 1971).

Aluminum frame assembly is
fast and easy: no tools are
needed; just insert clips
in the corner castings and
slip the castings into the
aluminum extrusions and the
frame is completed. By using any length of leg supports you can raise the
screen to the desired height.

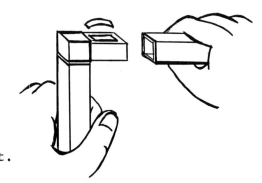

The drawing below illustrates the finished screen frame with
six foot leg supports and floor braces. The total cost of
the frame is under $50.

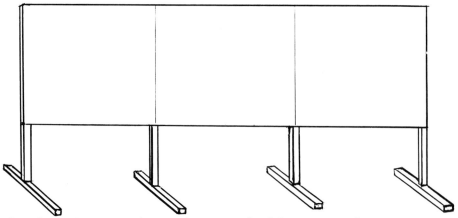

On the next page is a picture of this screen in use at a
workshop with religious educators. The images are rear-pro-
jected.

SCREEN MATERIALS

Media work with various communities and groups of people requires flexibility and mobility. It is important to have screens and frames that are durable and easily assembled.

There are many kinds of screens and screen material available at various prices. The permanently pressed bed sheet makes a very satisfactory and economical screen for both front and rear projection. With normal care the sheets will stay wrinkle-free when stretched across the frame. They are strong and can be washed when soiled.

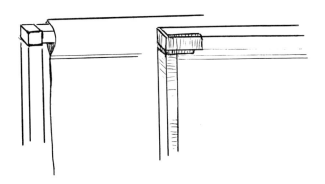

In the diagram at the left, the aluminum extrusion has been passed through the hem of the sheet prior to joining the corner casting with the side extrusion. The sheet is then stretched taut and taped to the side and bottom frames.

Part 5

THE MIX OF MEDIA

The sounds of dawn grow softly as a sunrise film breaks
through the deep colors of the overhead projections.

The art of blending the media to work as one unit is the art
of bringing together a new spectrum of awareness so that we
are able to experience something from many points of view.
The senses of touch, smell and taste are involved as well as
sight and sound. Like a collage, the possibilities and vari-
ations for expression become limitless when a mix of slide
and filmic images inter-weave with fluid light, sound or movement.

The shape that the Media Mix will take depends upon the sensitivity and artistry of the designer. The following pages show
some interesting co-expressions which we have used in celebrations.

When planning a script using multi-media there are two elements
to keep in mind:

> foreground (F.G.) that which is most prominent and
> commands attention. This could be a
> speaker, dancer, a film or musical com-
> position.

> background (B.G.) that which surrounds and supports
> the main images or character. The B.G.
> sets the environment so that the F.G. can
> have added meaning and impact.

In working with the Media Mix it is a good idea to try out the
ideas on groups of people in a workshop situation. Find out
which elements dominate, which ones seem weak. Determine what
is foreground and what is background. Sometimes it is necessary
to modulate or simplify parts.

> In a workshop with seminarians in Chicago we asked
> the young people to prepare five minute statements
> about "Something I want to stake my life on". Most
> of the first attempts seemed disjointed. The sound
> track and the visual images just did not work as a
> unit. During the rest of the year we continued to
> pursue the art of Media Mix. The growth in percep-
> tion and artistic sense was amazing. Proficiency
> in the blend of media was developed through regular
> creating sessions.

GENESIS THROUGH MIX-MEDIA

This section is a script based on <u>Genesis One</u> which we have
used in workshops as a way of giving people a feel for doing
MIX-MEDIA—a bringing together of many media languages to express a common message from many perspectives.

A group of 25 to 50 people wil be needed in order to do this
effectively. They can be arranged in the following creating
clusters:

<u>Visual Team</u>

      Members: 6-10 people
      Minimal Equipment: 2 overhead projectors
                             3 carousel projectors
                             spotlights on dimmer

<u>Sound Team</u>

      Members: 15 or more people
      Equipment: piano, primitive instruments,
                    bottles, etc.

<u>Drama Team</u>

      Members: 6-10 people
      Equipment: special lighting for black-out
                    scenes

<u>Dance Team</u>

      Members: 10 or more people
      Equipment: bodies

<u>Organizing for "Genesis One"</u>

The space where this will take place should be arranged with
screens and projectors proir to the assembling of the groups.
When the people gather, distribute sheets with the creation
script. Explain the idea of utilizing MIX-MEDIA to interpret
or "create" this portion of Scripture.

The following is an edited script:

GENESIS ONE

For a beginning God created the heavens and the earth. The earth was a formless void, there was darkness over the deep, and God's spirit was moving over the water.

God said, "Let there be light," and there was light.

God saw that the light was good, and God divided the light from the darkness. He called the light "day" and the darkness he called "night". Evening came and morning came: the first day.

God made the firmament and separated the waters which were under the firmament from the waters which were above the firmament. And God called the firmament "heaven". Evening came and morning came: the second day.

God said, "Let the waters under the heavens be gathered together into one place, and let the dry land appear." And it was so. And God called the dry land "earth", and the waters that were gathered together he called "seas".

God said, "Let the earth produce vegetation: plants yielding seed and fruit trees bearing fruit in which is their seed, each according to its kind, upon the earth." Evening came and morning came: the third day.

God said, "Let there be lights in the vault of heaven to divide day from night, and let them indicate festivals, days and years." And so it was. God made the two great lights: the greater light to govern the day, and the smaller light to govern the night and to divide light from darkness. God saw that it was good. Evening came and morning came: the fourth day.

God said, "Let the waters teem with living creatures, and let birds fly above the earth within the vault of heaven." And so it was. God blessed them saying, "Be fruitful, and multiply, and fill the waters of the seas; and let the birds multiply upon the earth." Evening came and morning came: the fifth day.

DRAMA BLACK-OUTS:

God said, "Let us make man in our own image, in the likeness of ourselves, and let them be masters of the fish of the sea,

the birds of heaven, the cattle, all the wild beasts and all
the reptiles that crawl upon the earth."

And God saw all that he had made, and indeed it was very good.
Evening came and morning came: the sixth day.

On the seventh day God completed the work he had been doing.
God blessed the seventh day.

And the horizon of Love is the meaning of the eighth day.

The Team Work of "Genesis One"

— read through the script with the entire group. Ask
for ideas on interpretation through visuals, sound,
drama and movement.

— explain what each team might do and have the people
select a creating group. The groups then assemble
in various rooms to begin working.

— each team works for about a half hour with an enabler
to organize their part of Genesis. Teams work through
timing and practice sequences.

— re-gather the groups and discuss the script again to
find out what each team is doing and when they will
enter in.

For instance, the Visual Team will interpret the
phrase, "Let there be light". The enabler would
need to know if other teams were also interpreting that phrase so that when the Narrator reads
the phrase, appropriate timing could be worked out.

— share Genesis One. A discussion might be desired after
the experience. However, very often the experience has
such depth that talking seems to trivialize the meaning.
The mood of the group at the closing of the experience
should be the deciding factor in whether or not a discussion is meaningful.

A WORD TO EACH OF THE TEAM

Visual Team

The role of the Visual Team is to provide an environment in which the other teams can be expressive. They will coordinate overhead projectors, slide projectors and any film equipment.

You will need to prepare beforehand some of the transparencies for the overheads which give a fluid feeling and a variety of slides portraying images of creation. Avoid being <u>illustrative</u> (i.e., when God creates the small animals, don't put on slides of little animals). Be imaginative.

You will probably use fluid light techniques more than slides. So, the Visual Team should be prepared for dimming and changing techniques on the overhead.

The team will have to listen to the Narrator for changes of light. Let the light environment begin slowly during the "void and formless" and pick up intensity and tempo as light is created. They will have to be flexible enough to sense mood changes in the total group when they are creating <u>Genesis One.</u>

Sound Team

This team will need to develop two kinds of sounds:

> <u>foundational sounds</u>: those which can be utilized at any point in <u>Genesis One</u> to avoid "sound gaps". Such sounds would be a flute or woodwind playing in a low register, in a meditative mood, or voices in a chanting sound on the vowels "u-e", or voices forming a chant on the sound "ah", or humming.

> <u>occasional sounds</u>: those which illustrate certain portions of <u>Genesis One</u>, such as the waters, living creatures, birds, etc.

The enabler who coordinates this team will have to utilize the imagination of the participants. The following listing contains some particularly memorable sound suggestions which people have made in workshops:

- a soloist begins singing the first and last verses of Psalm 90 as a prelude.

- the choir creates a breathy sound using empty pop bottles as the "Spirit of God moves over the waters".

- "Let there be light"— applauding and cheering.

- watery sounds— strumming the strings of a piano while pressing the sustaining pedal.

- "put forth vegetation"— vocal "bing bing" sounds like steel coils springing.

- "swarms of living creatures, birds"— these are obvious sounds.

- "make man in our image"— striking the chest in a heart-beat effect.

- "have dominion over" — marching sounds of feet

- the closing uses the choir gradually singing a familiar song such as, "All Creatures of Our God and King".

It will be important to establish a <u>flow</u> between each segment. Also, remember the importance of <u>silence as sound</u>.

Dance Team

The team enabler begins by loosening up the people so that each one feels the naturalness of movement and the simple rhythms of the body. It will be important to communicate that if creation is to have meaning it must happen <u>within</u> each dancer and not be something external.

Here are some suggested exercises for <u>moving Genesis One</u>:

- Invite the people to loosen up. Get out all the kinks.

Relax and lay on the floor so that no one is touch-
ing another person. (The lighting in the room should
be low, perhaps candle light.) Close the eyes. Begin to sense the life forces moving through you.

Imagine that you arelying in a primeval ooze. Begin
to feel your energies gathering. Can you sense the
struggle to remove yourself from this ooze?

As you rise, begin to experience the space around you.
No longer are you formless and void. Become an energy that calls you into life. "And the Spirit of God
was moving across the water."

— Now explore the energy of water. Using the arms and
back in a standing position become the waves of the
waters that covered the earth.

— Experience the movement of plant life, of seeds
growing. How does this movement differ from the
movement of water?

Each person could be a seed within a shell. Lying
on the floor, the "seeds" begin to grow, sinking
roots down deep and sending shoots through the
ground into the light.

— "And let there be light to separate the day and the
night." What kind of movement suggests the radiating light of day breaking through the darkness?
What kind of movement suggests the moon and the stars?

You might use two groups for this one. One group
being the light of day, and the second group being
the light of night. Coordinate this with the light
team.

— "Swarms of living creatures". Don't try to be too
literal at this point. Have the people choose an
animal, fish, bird, etc., and enact this creature
without using sound. Concentrate on the movement.

Suggest that they feel the inner energy of the animal.

Once the team has gone through these parts, you will have the task of figuring out how one movement flows into another. Take your time with the movements. Don't feel hurried. When the whole group assembles to re-check the script, communicate whatever effects are needed for the other groups. Also communicate to the Narrator where there is a need to pause in the script, in order to have enough time to move.

Drama Team

This team begins by exploring the conditions and situations of man. The format will be that of "black-out photo flashes"— sculpture-like frozen images which remain visible for about 8 seconds. The lights go out and a new sculpting is formed. Lights go on for another 8 seconds. This is repeated several times until about 5 or 6 sketches have been completed. Here are some possibilities:

Man is birth . . .

Man is fun . . .

Man is work . . .

Man is hatred . . .

Man is love . . .

Man is death . . .

Man is re-birth . . .

The drama team will need to rehearse how they move from one scene to another quickly. There may be some sketches which involve only a few members of the team, while other sketches would involve the whole group. The ideas should be discussed with the Light Team. Utilize, as much as possible, the sounds which the Sound Team could produce.

The Narrator

This person is like the conductor of an orchestra. He or she will determine how quickly or slowly the teams move through Genesis One. The narrator will have to notate on the script what and where the various teams will be creating. Pauses should also be noted.

SCRIPTING FOR LIGHT

In July, 1972, The Center enabled a celebration workshop with young people in Midland, Texas. Working with Sister Adelaide and myself was Rev. Fred Kingston from British Columbia. Fred utilizes spotlighting techniques in celebration and is able to achieve deeply moving moods with his artistry.

The celebration concluded a four-day workshop with 150 young people. More than 400 people attended the last evening's sharing. Fred used a "circle of light" for the main area of drama and speaking. The "circle" was achieved by placing three spotlights on the ceiling directly above the area and four spotlights on the walls to enlarge the light space. The "circle" fell directly in front of a free-standing screen which allowed for both front and rear projecting. The back wall had been covered with newsprint paper, making it an additional projecting surface.

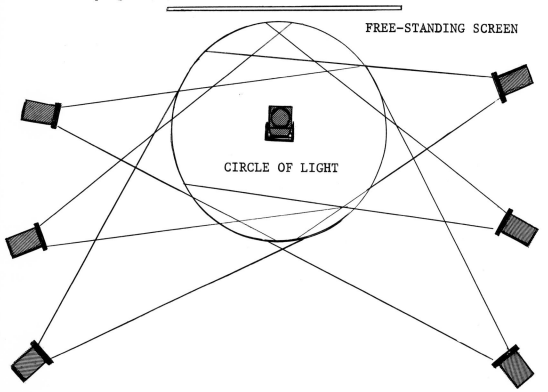

FREE-STANDING SCREEN

CIRCLE OF LIGHT

View from the ceiling looking down at the floor. Each spotlight was suspended 30 to 50 feet above the floor.

WORKSHOP CELEBRATION SCRIPT

The following is a simple working script from the Midland,
Texas celebration. The left side of the page refers to the
movement and development of the celebration. The right side
of the page gives the lighting techniques and effects used.

LITURGY	LIGHT
People enter and are greeted. New songs are rehearsed with the community.	All lights up.
A solo voice sings Psalm 90.	Lights slowly dim. Only a candlelight remains to read by.
Narrator begins the creation story from Genesis. The sound choir slowly evolves the music of creation as the dancers begin moving.	Overhead and slide projections visually evolve creation.
The "sun" dances in shadow behind the free-standing screen.	The "sun" is an amber light which slowly brightens from behind the free-standing screen.
With the creation of man, the drama team begins a series of "black-outs" in which the people mime man's possibilities for love, fun, hate, tension, birth and death, then re-birth.	Black-outs. All lights go out after each sketch. The photoflash poses are illuminated for 8 sec.

LITURGY	LIGHT
Celebrant concludes creation and invites people to join in the first song "CELEBRATE THE LIFE" which was composed by the young people.	Project words to song using overhead projector.
Celebrant leads meditation on our involvement in creation. People are invited to let their hands become the growing seeds. Two people come from the community to dialogue on "What keeps you growing?"	Spotlights on celebrant and speaker.
Each person in the congregation is invited to dialogue on the same question.	Lights gradually come up so that people can see one another.
Celebrant leads a prayer which is formed by the congregation.	Lights grow brighter as prayer concludes.
In groups of five or six the people design to show what keeps them growing as a people. Young people pass out packets of glue, scissors, felt and scrap material. The people work for about ten minutes. Soft guitar music is played in the background. People speak about the meaning of the banners. Banners are gathered by a team of people.	Lights up full.

LITURGY	LIGHT
Celebrant gathers people together with the song, "THE CHURCH WITHIN US" which is printed on song sheets.	Lights up full.
As the song concludes, freshly baked bread in warm bread pans is passed out to the community.	Lights begin to dim down.
Celebrant invites people to meditate on the broken-ness and the whole-ness of the bread they hold.	Soft spot light on speaker. Slides of hands breaking bread are projected on the screen.
Dramatic improvisation focuses the meaning of broken-ness in the world.	Circle of light. Bread slides go off the screen.
Celebrant leads communal meditation on the bread. A litany is formed spontaneously by the people. The bread is eaten following words of institution.	Soft single spotlight. Room is almost totally dark.
Sharing of the wine follows. More light was needed at this point so that the people could distribute the drink.	Lights gradually grow brighter.

LITURGY	LIGHT
Following the sharing of the wine the song "SONG OF THANKFULNESS" is sung from song sheets. The celebrant speaks about the church and the place celebration has in the future of the church. People are invited to give their "bread" so that young people and creativity can keep on. The money is received in the bread pans in which the bread had been baked.	Lights up full.
The many small banners which were made earlier in the service are now brought in on a large banner. This banner is six by ten feet and contains all the pieces and expressions of the community worked into a giant flower shape. The band plays an original song to celebrate the banner.	Room darkens so that banner can be spotlighted.

The benediction is sung:
 	
    "Move out the life that's singing in you.
    Live out the Spirit growing in you."
	The words are projected on the free standing screen from an overhead.

The band plays, people sing and dance.	Add slide projections and fluid lights.

Part 6

DESIGNING FOR CELEBRATION

Celebration Grows From Experience—Not From Themes

Celebration has an originating, organizing quality to it that
becomes a series of transforming episodes. Our experiences
break through with clearer understanding. To originate this
kind of meaning depends on our ability to probe experience:

> What were the shaping energies of this experience?
> What new form might this experience take in a
> religious depth?

It is important to let daily experience become one foundation
for designing celebration. Within each person's history of
experience, there is a wealth of insight into the meaning of
being human. How can we begin to uncover this meaning?

Many people, in their eagerness to develop celebration, begin
at the wrong place. Instead of exploring experience, they
select a theme and then try to illustrate it. Perhaps this
is still a hang-over from our early education when themes were
assignments for writing.

The difficulty with a theme is that in order to illustrate it,
we have to cut down the fullness of the experience to make it
fit the topic. We compromise meaning. Sometimes we may not
have any "feel" for the topic. Then celebration becomes the
type of forced labor that characterizes last minute term papers.

> A youth group was asked to do a Sunday morning
> worship service. They began by selecting the
> themes of "brotherhood" and "love"—fine senti-
> ments, but extremely over-used. What meanings
> do these words have for this youth group? In-
> stead of searching out their own experience
> they did a paste and scissors mix of prayers,
> recordings, readings and a few well-worn folk
> hymns.
>
> Where was the place for the uniqueness of person
> to come through?

Celebration's beginning
is with
PEOPLE—
using their
SHARED EXPERIENCES
and IDEAS

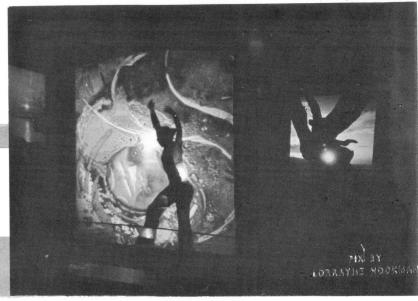

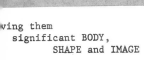ving them
significant BODY,
SHAPE and IMAGE

And memorable
SOUND-SPIRIT

> Following the service both adults and young people
> expressed appreciation for the effort but admitted
> that the service really didn't say anything new.

By simply illustrating a theme we run the risk of perpetuating
mass culture clichés and worn slogans (which at one time were
filled with real meaning until they became part of everyone's
with-it-ness language). Celebration thrives on the freshening
statement—using words which have an originating quality shaped
for a particular occasion.

The need to explore the meanings of experience is also very
important when developing celebrations around festive events
of Christian existence.

> "But," you may ask, "Christmas, Easter, Pentecost—
> aren't these themes?"

> "No. These are <u>environments</u>."

We need to recall always that the Christian journey through
time has been foundationed on man's experiencing of God's
Presence. If we are going to design a celebration of the
Christmas event, we must look freshly each year at the event
of Christmas in our living. Christmas is not a theme. It is
an event environment in which our history and heritage merge
with life situations today. Easter is the same. It is not
a theme to illustrate, but an event in the journey of our
tradition through which we explore the meaning of contemporary
experience.

Sometimes the situation arises where a specific group requests
a celebration designed around a certain theme. Our group from
The Center had this task laid on us when the General Synod of
the United Church of Christ asked us to design a communion
celebration around the Synod theme, "Whole Earth-Whole People".

We began by asking ourselves —what does 'whole earth' or
'whole people' mean? Or, what might it mean for the 3,000 del-
egates from around the country? Or, what is our experience of
"whole-ness" and where have we felt <u>whole</u> with people, with
earth? We also explored the other side of wholeness—broken-
ness—to see what this view could tell us.

We had to use our own experiences as models for this celebration.
We searched through Scripture to feel where the moments of whole-
ness and brokenness were present with the pioneers of the church.
Most important, we kept asking and imagining: What is this going
to mean to the people who attend? (Crucial to celebration is
the constant awareness of the meaning that you are trying to put
across and how this meaning might be received by people who have
not been part of the planning and preparation.)

It was important in this communion celebration to have a strong
visual image that could integrate the idea of wholeness-broken-
ness and people-earth. This image, which was most memorable,
came in the shape of nearly one hundred loaves of bread—all
kinds and shapes—from around the world.

What Is A Centering Image and Why Is One Needed in Celebration?

Each of us has a wealth of daily experiences which we order in a way that shapes who we are. The church, with a wealth of experiences and significant events, also gives particular shape to these meanings. Often these meanings take symbolic expression—gesture, the cross, colors.

A celebration also needs <u>one memorable image</u> around which the service can radiate and grow. We stress the one memorable image, since in designing a celebration, we might have four or five important images, which, if they were all used, would be confusing. People would go away in a sea of images. They may not remember anything from the service which employs a scatter-gun technique.

A centering image, such as the loaves of bread from around the world, helps us to get below the flow of ideas and experiences. It stimulates our imagination. We come down on what it is that runs as a common thread through these multi-dimensional, multi-faceted events. The centering image pulls the whole together and gives us a depth direction from which tangents can radiate.

The centering image grows after we have explored the experiences of our people. It becomes the <u>thematic motif</u> which <u>organizes the whole</u> and permits the people to <u>flow from the center to the parts</u>.

> In a recent workshop at Marshall University, West Virginia, forty participants expressed themselves in tremendously creative ways—original lyrics, slides, movement, sound. We planned to share this creativity in a celebration with other members of the community and families in a Sunday morning celebration.
>
> But how can the creativity of forty people be organized so that it is not a "show and tell" time or an "audio-visual demonstration" of newly acquired techniques?
>
> The people suggested some possibilities for organizing image—
>
>> loneliness being overcome
>> creativity
>> freedom to express myself
>> meeting new people

These were not the centering images. They were
the immediate images, reporting what our experiences were. They did not have the quality of the
common thread that brings meaning out of what we
were about.

Sister Adelaide and I worked into the night after
the 10 p.m. workshop concluded. We reviewed the
content and meanings of songs, visuals and script
ideas. We were still immersed in the immediacy of
the day. Our task was to pull away from the experience and get a total view of the pulsing going
on in the people.

We worked until 2 a.m. and came up with a lot of
ideas and possible images, such as the growth of a
seed, as a symbol of creation. Many of the ideas
were left-overs from previous celebrations. But
nothing was coming that felt right. So we called
it quits without having a fresh image that could
organize the morning's celebration.

At 7 a.m. we hit it again. During the few hours
of sleep we had, something broke through. Could
we celebrate the "potential within us"? There was
a great deal of potential among the people and a
real interest in carrying on. What we were sharing during these few days was the awakening potential within the people...a potential which was more
than the sum total of all the people together.

Later that morning more than 200 people gathered
from the university community to share in the celebration. To draw each person into the creating experience of the weekend, marble globs were given
to everyone and each person placed the glob into a
dish of water on the overhead projector. As more
people entered the room, the projected image which
had been a white light soon became filled in with
shimmering colors and shapes. This opening symbolized the uniqueness of each person in celebration
and that our time together involved all kinds and
styles of people's creativity.

The songs, dance and movement of the liturgy and communion took place within the visual context of "people together are endless possibilities". This phrase was written on clear slides and then projected on the walls using three carousel projectors.

The Shape Celebration Takes Is An Extension of a People

Just as a car extends the foot, a musical instrument extends the voice, a camera extends the eye, so celebration is a multidimensional extension of a people. The style of persons will determine the style and depth of celebration.

There's a real authenticity of celebration that grows out of a small group of people who have shared experiences together. Their celebration is a coming together of the mutual tunings which have formed this group. No one tries to impose a form because all present have participated in this forming. There is a common understanding of who they are as a people, what they are celebrating and who is doing the celebration. This style of celebration grows from the experiences of the group. The struggle and joy, the times of failure and success, the moments of anger and love will all be part of the network. There might be a place for the "seer" or theologian of the group to explore with depth the workings of this people, to draw upon the resources of the past which foundations this people in the present and to give shape to the future.

There is also a style of celebration which requires a gathering of the spirit of the people. This is quite often the situation of the local church on Sunday morning.

> How can we re-gather a people and realize that
> we are a new people?

> We've had a wealth of experiences since we were
> together last. Can we celebrate this newness?

Developing this style of celebration requires preparation by a team of people working with the minister. A team will need to be in tune with the significant stirrings of the congregation. They will need to have enough imaginative resources to determine centering images which have meaning for the people.

The <u>team</u> is <u>not a committee</u>. The team has momentum and does not need to be called into session by a chairman. There may be a coordinator but not a chairing person. In a team all the people are participants, creators and givers of direction to the plans and activities.

In most situations teams work best on <u>short term commitments</u>. A group of creative people do not seem to function fully when they are given repetitive tasks, such as planning a service week after week. To keep the momentum going a number of creative teams will have to be formed so that they can each handle the chores of a variety of different celebrations. Each team would be responsible for coming in with the research and ideas that could shape a design for your people.

The process through which styles of celebration move are still being developed and explored. Your own research and documentation of the ideas and events, failures and successes will be of great value as your work in celebration grows and deepens. Try to keep a journal of your experiences. If possible, tape record and photograph or film the celebrations you do.

God,
    give us the courage of prophets —
        to speak a language which may
    horrify some but liberate others,
grant us strength to be ourselves —
    (which at times may horrify
        some but liberate others)
fill us with wisdom to go and
    lighten the world —

EXPANDING RESOURCES

PHOTOGRAPHY

Life Library of Photography. Time-Life Books, New York, 1970. An excellent series on all aspects of photography.

Introduction to Photography. Robert B. Rhode & Floyd H. McCall, The Macmillan Company, New York, 1971.

The Complete Photographer. Prentice-Hall, Inc., Englewood Cliffs, New Jersey, 1966.

The Creative Photographer. Prentice-Hall, Inc. Englewood Cliffs, New Jersey, 1955.

Guidebooks by Kodak, Rochester, New York, 14650. A wide variety of interesting, easy to understand booklets dealing with almost every topic related to photomaking.

FILM MAKING

How to Shoot a Movie Story. Arthur L. Gaskill & David Englander, Morgan & Morgan Publishers, New York, 1960.

Creative Film-Making. Kirk Smallman, Collier Books, New York, 1969. Offers a good guide to film formats and materials as well as very readable material on animation and live film techniques. Well-illustrated.

Guide to Film-Making. Edward Pincus, New American Library, Signet Books, New York, 1969. An invaluable handbook that covers all topics for film-makers.

Children as Film-Makers. John Lidstone & Don McIntosh, Reinhold Company, New York, 1970. Hundreds of illustrations show every aspect of a real program that develops film-making in the classroom.

UNDERSTANDING VISUALS

The Audio-Visual Man. edited by Pierre Babin, George Pflaum, Dayton, Ohio, 1970. Deals clearly and concisely with many topics related to the use of media in religious education and liturgical services. Works to develop a sense of visual literacy in the reader.

Visualize. David R. Anderson and Gary Wilburn, George Pflaum, Dayton, Ohio, 1971. Offers four seminar workshop plans designed to develop visual skills. Deals with the purpose of visuals, a brief history of the film, the elements of film-making and multi-media production.

Environmental Man. William Kuhns, Harper & Row, New York, 1969. An analysis of the interaction between man and particular environments.

"Modern Media Teacher". 38 W. 5th Ave., Dayton, Ohio 45402.

LIGHTING

Edmund Unique Lighting Handbook. No. 9100. Edmund Scientific Co., Barrington, New Jersey 08007. 1969. A handbook that answers the needs of anyone wishing to produce a light show. Includes facts, ideas, techniques and suggestions regarding equipment.

"Theatre Crafts" Jan/Feb., 1970. Vol. 4, No. 1. 565 Fifth Ave., New York 10017. The entire issue is devoted to multi-media in theatre.

STAGE LIGHTING

Scenic Design and Stage Lighting. W. Oren Parker & Harvey K. Smith, Yale University, Holt, Rinehart and Winston, Inc., New York, 1963. Part III, on lighting, begins with principles of electricity and lighting instruments, goes on to analyze the equipment needs of educational and community producing groups. Professional approach encouraged.

Simplified Stagecraft Manual. Leroy Stahl, T.S. Denison & Company, Inc., Minneapolis, 1962.

Stage Scenery and Lighting. 3rd ed. Samuel Selden & Hunton D. Sellman, Appleton-Century-Crafts, Inc., New York, 1959. Basic professional lighting.

American Documentary Films
336 W. 84th Street
New York   10024
        or
379 Bay Street
San Francisco, CA 94133

Argus Communication
3505 N. Ashland Ave.
Chicago, Ill.   60657

Cathedral Films, Inc.   (Religious and educational
2921 W. Alameda   films and filmstrips)
Burbank, CA   91505

Center Cinema Co-op   (Library of films. Cooperative
Columbia College   of underground film makers)
Chicago, Illinois

Concordia Films
3558 S. Jefferson Ave.
St. Louis, MO   63118

Contemporary Films   (Short Subjects, Documentaries,
McGraw-Hill Book Co.   National Film Board of Canada
   Midwest - 828 Custer Ave.   films)
      Evanston, Ill. 60202
   East - 276 W. 25th Street
      New York   10001
   West - 1211 Poly St.
      San Francisco, CA 96209

Creative Film Society   (Creative short subjects, docu-
14558 Valerio Street   mentary, experiments and abstract
Van Nuys, CA   91405   films)

Film and Art
554 Lexington St.
Waltham, Mass.   02154

Franciscan Communications Center
1229 S. Santee Street
Los Angeles, CA   90015

LaSalle Catechetical Center
3501 Solly Ave.
Philadelphia, PA 19136

(Provides religion educators
with good AV materials for use
in various educational and
liturgical settings)

National Audio-Visual
  Association, Inc.
3150 Spring Street
Fairfax, VA 22030

(Clearing house. Sponsors con-
ventions and offers materials)

New Life Films
Box 2008
Kansas City, Kansas 66110

("Visual and Verbal Meditations"
  Slides and script)

Travarca
Box 247
Grandville, Michigan 49418

(Film rental)

WBBM-TV Film Loan Library
630 N. McClur Court
Chicago, Illinois 60611

(Television documentaries and
  public affairs programs)

SUPPLIERS OF SPECIAL ITEMS

American Science Center, Inc.
5700 Northwest Highway
Chicago, Illinois 60646

(Science items, Optics, Space,
  Unique lighting effects)

Photo Plastic International
P.O. Box 2868
Culver City, CA 90230

(Film slide mounts, Album pages)

INDEX